HAJJ & UMRAH ACCORDING TO ALL FOUR SCHOOLS OF JURISPRUDENCE

Also by Qazi Fazl Ullah

Sharia & Politics

Science of Hadith

Jesus in the Quran

Jihad: Why, How, & When

Sayyidah Aaisha: Age & Marriage

Ramadan: Components of the Holy Month

HAJJ & UMRAH ACCORDING TO ALL FOUR SCHOOLS OF JURISPRUDENCE

WRITTEN BY **QAZI FAZL ULLAH**
EDITED BY **EVELYN THOMPSON**

HUND INTERNATIONAL PUBLISHING

LOS ANGELES, CALIFORNIA

2022

COPYRIGHT © 2022 BY QAZI FAZL ULLAH

All rights reserved. This book or any portion thereof may not be reproduced or used in any manner whatsoever without the express written permission of the publisher except for the use of brief quotations in a book review or scholarly journal.

FIRST PRINTING: 2022

ISBN: 978-1-970049-27-5

HUND INTERNATIONAL PUBLISHING

LOS ANGELES, CALIFORNIA

PRINTED IN THE UNITED STATES OF AMERICA

Table of Contents

PREFACE	13
INTRODUCTION	15
A FEW AHADITH REGARDING HAJJ AND SOME PLACES THEREIN	20
THE MEANING OF *ISTITA'A*	32
UMRAH	36
CONDITIONS OR PRE-REQUISITES OF *HAJJ* AND *UMRAH*	39
HAJJ UL BADAL (*HAJJ* ON BEHALF OF ANOTHER)	48
THE CONDITIONS FOR *HAJJ UL BADAL*	58
MAWAQEET	66
MEEQAT (THE APPOINTED PLACE)	69

UMRAH (AL HAJJ UL ASGHAR)	80
THE CONTENTS OF *UMRAH*	81
HAJJ	91
HAJJI TAMATTU	94
HAJJI QIRAN	95
FARD IN *HAJJ*	105
1. *IHRAM*	105
1. *WUQUF* AT *ARAFAH*	113
2. *TAWAF*	118
HOW TO DO *TAWAF*?	124
SHURUT OF *TAWAF*	125
IMPORTANT ISSUES REGARDING WOMEN IN *HAJJ*	130
SUNNAH OF *TAWAF*	132

SAI	137
WAJIBAT OF *HAJJ*	140
WUQUF AT *MUZDALAFAH*	143
STAY AT *MINA* AND *RAMI*	148
SHAVE/TRIM	156
ZAB'H	160
TAWAF UL WIDA	165
SUNNAH OF *HAJJ* AND *UMRAH*	166
RESTRICTIONS IN *IHRAM*	170
COMPENSATION FOR *JINAYAT*	179
MISSING A *WAJIB* AND ITS COMPENSATION	189
MISSING *HAJJ* AFTER *IHRAM*	194

IHSAR OR CEASURE FROM *HAJJ*	196
TRIP TO *MEDINA*	199
BOOKS BY *QAZI FAZL ULLAH*	202
ABOUT THE AUTHOR	217

PREFACE

Hajj, or pilgrimage to *Makkah* (*Mecca*, located in *Saudi Arabia*), is one of the five pillars of *Islam*. Most people perform *Hajj* only once in their lifetime, so they do not have a chance to become accustomed to its complexities. They follow different practices dictated by the *Prophet Muhammad Ibn Abd Allah* (Peace Be Upon Him). Moreover, various jurists have preferred certain customs over the years. Other *Muslims* think what these jurists are doing is wrong, as they have been taught differently. Sometimes they start arguing with one another and even come to blows during what is supposed to be a peaceful gathering of the faithful. In fact, the universality of *Ibadah* (submission to *Allah*) demands that all *Hajj* practices must be equally honored.

In *Hajj*, there are different issues where one *imam* has adopted a slightly stricter way than another. Also, the eminent *Ulama* (scholars) do not allow or recommend *Talfeeq* (combining opinions) and *Tashah'hi* (switching from one *imam* to another depending on the issue), but it does happen. We have tried our best to mention all these four well-known *Mazahib* of *Ahlus-Sunnah* regarding *Hajj* and its *Manasik*, keeping in mind that none of them has said anything from their own; they only interpret, explain or apply a verse, a *Hadith*, or an *Athar* of a *Sahabi*. An authentic *Mufti* of a *Madhab* can issue a *Fatwa* to someone on a particular issue in a particular situation, even according to the decree of another *Imam* other than his own. That *Fatwa* may be for that individual on that particular issue for that time only. It may not be generalized to include others or even to the same person the next time, as it may lead towards *Tashah'hi* and *Talfeeq*.

May *Allah* accept it and keep us on the right path. *Amin*!

QAZI FAZL ULLAH

LOS ANGELES, CALIFORNIA USA

INTRODUCTION

Islam is the *Deen* of *Allah*, *Deen* of all the messengers and prophets and the *Deen* of all humanity. This *Deen* started with *Adam*, and continued with *Noah* (*Nuh*), *Abraham* (*Ibrahim*), *Moses* (*Musa*), and *Jesus* (*Isa*). It was completed with the last and final *Prophet* of *Allah*, *Prophet Muhammad*. Peace be upon all the *Messengers* and *Prophets* of *Allah*. The core tenets of *Islam*, its concept of worship, and its codes of ethics are one and the same. However, the details are different according to the different times of these messengers and the situations they and their people were living in.

The five pillars of *Islam* are a declaration of faith, daily prayer, fasting at *Ramadan*, tithing, and a pilgrimage to *Makkah*. Historically, there were two *Qiblas* (directions) for the purpose of prayer: The *Bait Ul Maqdas* (near the *Dome of the Rock* in *Jerusalem*) and the *Baitullah* (the *Ka'ba* in *Mecca*). However, for the purpose of *Hajj*, there is only one place and that is *Baitullah*, the first ever house built upon the earth for the benefit of human beings in general:

> *"Indeed, the first ever house laid down (on the earth) for people is the one in "Bakkah" (Makkah), a blessed one and a guidance for all worlds (3:96 Holy Quran)."*

Legend has it that this house was first built by the angels. However, being in a valley, it was flooded and destroyed several times and built up by different people. The *Holy Quran* mentions the building of *Prophet Abraham* (*Ibrahim*):

> *"And remember when Abraham (Ibrahim) was raising up the foundations of the house and Ishmael (Ismail) as well (2:127 Holy Quran)."*

The current building is said to have been raised by *Hajjaj Ibni Yusuf*. However, it has been rebuilt or repaired many times since.

It is no coincidence that the site the house of *Allah* lies along the real Date Line and Magnet Line. It is also said to be the center of gravity as well.

Allah said

"In this there are several clear signs from theses (one) is Maqami Ibrahim (3:97 Holy Quran)."

These clear signs are few, but *Allah* mentioned one, i.e., *Maqam-E-Ibrahim* (a stone where the feet of *Ibrahim / Abraham* were imprinted when building the House). We know and believe the spirituality of these signs. However, besides that there are signs scientifically proving that this a center of the spiritual world.

The water of the *Zamzam* Well, located near the *Ka'ba*, is full of nutrients and minerals. It has been scientifically proven that the water in *Makkah* (*Mecca*) contains 260 milligrams of useful contents per liter, while one liter from the Well has 2000 mg.

The *Prophet* of *Allah* said:

This [the water] *is food, and this is healing.*

The black stone in the *Ka'ba*, also known as *Hajari Aswad*, was said by the Prophet to have come from *Jannah*, heaven. Scientifically it is proven that this kind of stone is not found anywhere in the world. These are only a few examples. There are innumerable benefits for those who go to *Mecca*:

> *"So, they may witness benefits for them (22:28 Holy Quran)."*

Ibadat (worship) connotes obedience in devotion. However, there is so much wisdom in *Ibadat* as well. *Ibadat* brings one closer to *Allah*.

Allah said:

> *"And seek towards Allah the means/source (to take you near to Him) (5:34 Holy Quran)."*

The closer one is to *Allah*; the humbler becomes one's shape and situation of one.

When a *Hajji* (Pilgrim) is in *Ihram* (the sacred state of pilgrimage), he or she is not allowed to cut nails or hair, or put on perfume. He or she disconnects from worldly concerns, fully occupied with *Ibadah*, as a type of retreat for *Allah*.

Ibadat is of three types:

a) Verbal and oral

b) Physical

c) Financial rituals

The *Hajj* is a combination of all three types.

Hajj is *Fard* (duty) for those who can afford it:

> *Moreover, for Allah, there is Hajj of the House upon people (i.e., one who can afford to go) (3:97 Holy Quran).*

A FEW AHADITH REGARDING HAJJ AND SOME PLACES THEREIN

HAJJ

1. Ali narrated that the prophet said,

    "whoever owned a ride and expenses which can take him to the house of Allah, but he did not perform Hajj, then there is nothing on him but to do as a Jew or Christian" (Tirmizi)

2. *Ibni Abbas* related from the *Prophet* of *Allah* that he said,

    "Whoever has wealth which can take him to the house of Allah, or zakat became incumbent on him but he didn't do that, he will ask for a go back to this world at the time of death." (Kanzul Ummal)

3. *Ibni Abbas* said from the *Prophet* of *Allah* that said,

    "Whoever intended Hajj, he should hurry up" (*Abu Dawud*)

4. Abu Saeed said, that the *Prophet* said from *Allah* that he says,

A slave whom I have perfected for him his body (health) and enlarged his living (means), if five years passed on him and he did not come to me (my house for Hajj or Umrah) is indeed deprived (of my mercy). (Ibni Hiban)

5. *Ibni Shammasah*, says we visited *Amr Ibnul Aas* at the time of his death so he cried and said,

   When Allah put (the love of) Islam in my heart, I said, o the messenger of Allah I want to put a condition. He said go ahead, what? I said don't you know o Amr! Verily Islam demolishes whatever was before if and "Hijrah"(leaving one's own homeland for Allah) demolishes whatever was before that and hajj demolishes whatever was before that (means it wipes out the sins). (Ibni Khuzaimah)

6. *Buraidah* said that the *Prophet* of *Allah* said,

   "To spend in hajj is like spending in the path of Allah (means in jihad) to 700 times." (Ahmad, Tabrani)

7. *Ibni Asud* said, the *Prophet* said,

> *"Constantly perform Umrah and Hajj as these two take away sins and poverty like the furnace takes away the rust of iron, silver, and gold."* (*Bayhaqi*)

8. Also *Jabar* says, the *Prophet* said *Bayhaqi* related from *Aaisha* that the *Prophet* said,

   "Verily the angels will shake hands with those who comes for hajj on ride and will hug those who come on foot."

9. *Ibni Majah* narrated from *Abu Hurairah* that the *Prophet* said,

   Those who perform Hajj and Umrah are the delegates of Allah, if they invoke Allah he responds and of ask him the forgiveness he forgives.

10. *Al Bazzar* narrated from *Abu Hurairah* that

    "A Hajj is intercession would be accepted in favor of 400 people of his family ad he comes out of his sins like the day the mother delivered him."

11. *Buraidah* said from the *Prophet*

    "And when you met a Haji say Salam to him, shake hands with him and ask him

to ask forgiveness for you as he is a forgiven one." (*Ahmad*)

12. *Bukhari* and *Muslim* related from *Abu Hurairah* that the *Prophet* of *Allah* said,

    "Whoever performed Hajj and he did not take evil (therein) nor he did wrong, he goes back like the day his mother delivered him."

13. *Amr Ibni Abasah* narrated from the *Prophet*, he said ,

    "The best of the deeds is Hajj-i-Mabrooh or umrah Mabrooh" (*Ahmad, Tabrani*)

    Mabroor means which is performed in its proper way without violations.

14. *Abu Hurairah* said,

    a Umrah to another Umrah is an expiation for what was in between these two (Umrahs). (Bukhari, Muslim).

15. The *Prophet* said,

    "The Jihad is an old man and weak one and for a woman is Hajj and Umrah." (*Nisa'i* from *Abu Hurairah*).

Also *Aaisha* said, *I asked the permission for Jihad from the prophet, so he said your (means the women's) Jihad is Hajj.*

"All these rewards and virtues are for those who perform there Hajj and Umrah with full sincerity for the sake of Allah properly as Allah said and perform Hajj and Umrah for Allah properly" (2:196)

And the *Prophet* said,

A time is coming on people their rich will be performing Hajj for amusement, their, their Medueen type people will be doing it for business. Their poor will do it for begging and their "Qura" (Ulama and Qari) will be doing that for fame and show up."(Kanzul Ummal from Dee Lamis Musud).

16. *Abu Hurairah* said, the *Prophet* said,

When a haji depart with lawful wealth putting his put in the saddle and say "Labbaik" a caller calls him from the heaven "Labbaika Wa Sadaika" your wealth is lawful and your ride is also "Halal" and your hajj is bringing you a good and not a sin and when departs with and unlawful wealth and puts his foot in the saddle and says "Labbaik" a caller calls him from the heaven "la Labbaika Wa la Sadaika" your wealth is haram and your ride is unlawful and your hajj is "Mazoor" not "Mabroor". (Tabrani)

"*Mazoor*" is from "*Wizr*" which means sin or a burden on you.

Makkah: in *Quran* Allah called it "*Al Baladul Ameen*" and took an oath on it and said,

"and (I swear) by this city of security"(95:3)

Also he said

"I swear by this city and you are born in thus city" (9:12)

Also he ordered his *Prophet* to say

"I have been ordered to worship the lord of this city who has sanctioned it and the much more liked to him" (27:91)

Umar said,

To commit to sins at Rukya (a place) is tolerable to me than committing one at Makkah (Kanzul Ummal)

It means that one sin at Makkah is too much than sins in other places.

Allah said

> *"And whoever intended therein profanity (or sin) wrongfully (unjustly) we will cause him to taste of the formant of a blazing fire" (22:25)*

Baitullah (the house of *Allah*): *Ibni Abbas* said the *Prophet* of *Allah* said,

> *"Verily from Allah there are one hundred twenty mercies coming down to this house (of Allah), sixty for those who are making tawaf and forty for those who pray there and twenty for those who are looking at it." (Bayhaqi, Maazani)*

In a *Hadith* it is said, that looking at the house of *Allah* is "*Ibadah*" (worship).

Hateem; its literal meaning is broken as this part which is in shape of almost half circle or bracket shape. This was inside the structure of the house of *Allah*, but kept out of it when *Quraish* were building it up.

At that time the age of the *Prophet* was thirty five years and he also took part in its construction with his uncle *Abbas* when that was the time of *Bani Hashim* to work. This was kept out because of the deficit in the budget.

Aaisha says,

I wished if I can enter the house of Allah and pray there. So the messenger of Allah took me to "Hateem" and said pray here when you wish to enter the house of Allah as this is a part of the house as your people (Quraish) fell short (of expenses) so they kept it out it." (Abu Dawud)

Hajari Aswad, this stone (rock) is originally from *Jannah* (paradise).

Ibni Abbas said, that the *Prophet* of *Allah* told us

"I swear by Allah, Allah will raise it on the day of resurrection, having two eyes looking with and a tongue talking with, testifying for you one who did its "Istilam" truly." (Tirmizi, Ibni Majah, Darimi)

Ibni Abbas also related from the *Prophet*

"That when it came from paradise it was whiter than milk" (Ahmad, Tirmizi)

Rukni Yamani – *Abu Hurairah* says that the *Prophet* said,

"Over Rukni Yamani there appointed 70,000 angels so whosoever said, Allahumma inni asalukal afwa wal aafiyata fid dunya wal aakhivah, rabbana aatina fid dunya hasanatanwa fil aakhirati hasanatanwa qina azban nar" they say "aamin" (Ibni Majah)

Multazam: that is the wall of *Kaba* in between the *Hajari Aswad* and the door of *Kaba*.

Ibni Abbas says, I heard the *Prophet*,

"He said Multazam is the place invocation is heard and accepted there. No slave invoke Allah there but he responds that." (Al Jazari, shah Waliullah)

Zamzam: this is the name of the well and its water as well. This water is naturally alkaline water in the whole world and the healthiest one.

Jabir said,

I heard the prophet, he said, water of Zamzam is for what is has been drank

(means for nutrition or for treatment). (Ibni Majah)

Some *Muhaditheen* criticized this *Hadith* and said "*Zaeef*" but *Ibni Hajar* said this is *Sahih*.

Umar said,

I drink it to quench my thirst on the day of resurrection. Also the prophet used to make a Dua after its drinking " o Allah bestow on me a beneficial provision and healing from every disease, knowledge excessed deeds pure (Halal).

10 days of *Zul Hijjah*: *Allah* said,

"By the dawn and by the 10 nights and by the even and the odd." (89:1,2,3)

By these 10 nights he meant the 10 nights of *Zul Hijjah*. *Ibni Abbas* says the *Prophet* said,

"No need in any days is better than the one in these days. They said, and not even jihad in the path of Allah? He said and not even jihad in the path of Allah, but only of one who went out (in this path) personally along with his wealth and didn't bring anything back (means neither his wealth nor his life but sacrificed both)." (Ahmad, Abu Dawud, Tirmizi, Ibni Majah).

Also by the even of the 10th of *Zul Hijjah* is meant as *Masrooq* said and by odd and even the 9th and 10th of *Zul Hijjah* is meant as *Jabir* narrated from the *Prophet* (*Ahmad, Nisa'i*). while *Ibni Zubair* said, it is the 12th and 13th of *Zul Hijjah* in line, which the *Hujjaj* throw the *Jamarat*.

Arafah and *Arafat*: *Arafa* in the name of the 9th of *Zul Hijjah* when *Hujjaj* stay there until sunset. That is the main "*Rukn*" of *Hajj*. the *Prophet* said "*Hajj* is *Arafah*" then this word title or term is used for that stay till it became famous for that more than the day.

1. *Aaisha* say from the messenger of *Allah*, he said,

   There is no other day but Arafat that Allah emancipate so many of his slaves from the fire, and verily he comes close (to them) and he rejoices because then in front of his angels saying, what are these people looking for? (Muslim)

2. *Talha Ibni Ubaidullah* says that the *Prophet* said,

   "Satan is never been seen in such a small rejected humiliated and angry as he is on the day of Arafah. And this is because of the mercy coming down and

forgiveness of sins except the day of Badr." (malik)

"*Talbiyah*" it means to say *Labbaik Allahumma....*

Sahl Ibni Sad says, the *Prophet* said

"No muslim says "Talbiyah" but everything to his right and left i.e the rocks, the trees, the mud says it up to the boundaries of the earth." (Tirmizi, Ibni Maja)

The *Prophet* was asked

What is a Haji? He said having disheveled hair and fall to dirt. They said and what is Hajj? He said the Hajj and "Haji" means the loud echo of Talbiyah and the blood shed (animal sacrifice).

THE MEANING OF *ISTITA'A*

Istita'a is the capability to perform *Hajj*. *Imam Malik* said, a pilgrim may conduct the *Hajj* in any lawful way he can manage. *Imam Shafi* said, that if one is in adequate health to travel and can afford the expense, s/he is obligated to perform *Hajj*. *Imam Abu Hanifa* said, one must not only be in good physical health but also must be able to provide for him or herself and any dependent family members as well. Thereby avoiding a situation where a pilgrim spends all he or she has to perform *Hajj* and is destitute afterward. *Imam Ahmad* says that one who has the means to travel to *Hajj* is bound to do so. As it is stated in a *Hadith* narrated by *Dari Qutni* from *Aisha*, *Jabir*, *Anas*, *Ibni Umar* and *Abdullah Ibni Amr*, the *Prophet* explained that whenever someone enters into the state of *Istita'a*, he or she should perform the *Hajj* as soon as possible. According to *Imam Abu Hanifa*, *Imam Malik*, and *Imam Ahmad*.

Ali related a *Hadith*:

Perform Hajj before that (time comes when) you cannot do it. (Hakim, Bayhaqi)

Ibni Abbas narrated from the *Prophet;*

"Hurry up for Hajj as no one knows what will happen to him (next year) (Ahmad and Abu Nuaim)."

One who is not affected by illness or an openly (known) need or an openly known hardship or by unjust authority and he did not perform Hajj. So he may die as a Jew or as a Christian as he wants (Ahmad, Bayhaqi, Abu Yala Saeed Ibni Mausoom).

Also, *Imam Tirmizi* related a *Hadith*:

Whoever owns needs and ride that can take him to the House of Allah, and he did not perform Hajj, so nothing is on him to die as a Jew or a Christian, and this is because

Allah said:

"And for Allah, this is incumbent on people to do Hajj of the House, whoever can afford to go."

The *Hadith* of *Abu Umamah* contains the phrase *"Falam Yahujja,"* with *FA* meaning *"soon."* However, *Imam Shafi* said, *Nafsi Wujub* has come with *Istita'a*. However, *Wujubi Ada* (to perform) is at one's convenience, but still one is to do it soon. He also says that *Hajj* became *Fard* in the 6Th year after *Hijra* and the *Prophet* delayed it to 10th year, which means a delay for personal reasons is permitted.

However, there is another opinion that it became *Fard* in the 9th year. The *Prophet* sent *Abu Bakr* as *Amir* that year and next year, he went himself. That delay was because of *Nasi,* which is a term that means the people of *Makkah* used to modify the calendar for their convenience. For example, if *Hajj* fell either in their business season or the harvest, or even in hot weather, they would change it, so the *Hajj* in the 9th year did not fall in *Zul Hijjah*. That is why the *Prophet* delayed the same to the next year, even if it was made *Fard* in the 6Th year, still that may be the reason for delay, and the *Prophet* in his *Khutbah* said:

> *The time [calendar] rotated to its [original] shape, the day Allah created the heavens and the earth.*

UMRAH

Umrah (pilgrimage to *Makkah* not the *Hajj's one*) is *Sunnah Muakkadah* (highly recommended) once in one's lifetime by *Imam Abu Hanifa* and *Imam Malik*. The legend is that a *Bedouin* came to the *Prophet* and said,

> *"Tell me about Umrah! Is it Wajib [mandatory]?" The Prophet said "no", but if you do it, that is good for you (Ahmad, Tirmizi, Bayhaqi, Ibni Abi Shaibah and Abd Ibni Hamaid).*

Tirmizi called it *Sahih*. However, in the narration chain, there is *Hajjaj Ibni Artat*, who is *Daeef*.

Dari Qutni and *Bayhaqi* quoted from *Abu Hurairah* that *Hajj* is *jihad*, and *Umrah* is recommended. However, *Ibni Hajar* said that there is a weakness in the narrative chain.

Imam Shafi and *Imam Ahmad* said *Umrah* is *Fard*, as *Allah* said:

"And perform Hajj and Umrah perfectly for Allah (2:196 Holy Quran)."

Ibni Maja and *Bayhaqi* state that *Aisha* (the *Prophet's* wife) asked the *Prophet*,

"Is there any jihad on women?"

The *Prophet* said,

"Yes, A jihad where there is no fighting in it: The Hajj and Umrah."

So, in the *Ayah* (verse) there is the commandment, which is binding, while in that *Ayah* and the *Hadith* both *Hajj* and *Umrah* are mentioned together in the same context, and as the *Hajj* is *Fard*, *Umrah* is therefore the same.

Also, it is quoted from *Imam Ahmad* that there is no *Umrah* on *Makkans* (residents of *Makkah*), as *Ibni Abbas* said,

"O people of Makkah! There is no Umrah on you, indeed, your Umrah is Tawaf,"

Which means,

"Umrah is Wajib, but not for the people of Makkah."

However, we say that not every commandment is *Wajib*. Some commandments are permissible only as mentioned in *"Jurisprudence"* in detail, so it depends, and as both are mentioned together, it does not necessarily mean they are similar in status. However, in performance perfectly, as *Allah* said, and also one can say '*Umrah* is *Sunnah*, so *Hajj* is *Sunnah*. So, what *Ibni Abbas* said it means,

> *That the big part of Umrah is Tawaf and you, the people of Makkah, are doing it anyway. So you do not need to go to Meeqat (the places at which pilgrims put on the white pilgrimage garment) even to Masjid e Tan'eem and to make intention for Umrah. So, we can say it means Umrah is not for you, the people of Makkah! For you, only Tawaf is enough.*

But according to three *Imams*, *Umrah* is for *Makkans* as well.

CONDITIONS OR PRE-REQUISITES OF *HAJJ* AND *UMRAH*

There are some requisites for *Hajj*:

1) ***ISLAM***

Only a *Muslim* is to perform the *Hajj*, according to *Imam Abu Hanifa*. Other *Imams* said that a non-*Muslim* is also the addressee of *Sharia* law but he or she cannot perform *Ibadat* because of his *Kufr* (non-belief).

2) **PUBERTY AND SENILITY**

The *Prophet* said:

The pen [binding] is dropped off of three - the sleeping one till he wakes up, the minor till he attains puberty, and the mad till he returns to sense (Abu Dawud and Ibni Majah).

Also, the *Prophet* said:

[If] the family of a minor arranged Hajj for a minor, then he [minor] died. It will

suffice him (for his Fard *Hajj). However, if he [the minor] attained puberty, there is Hajj on him (if he can afford), and if the master arranged Hajj for the slave. Then [if] he died it will suffice him, and if he is emancipated, then there is Hajj on him (if he can afford) (Imam Shafi and Saeed Ibni Mansoor).*

The *Hajj* of a mature minor is allowed, but it is not considered his *Fard Hajj*, according to *Imam Malik*, *Imam Shafi* and *Imam Ahmad* the custodian should do their intention. As *Ahmad*, *Muslim*, *Abu Dawud*, and *Nisa'i* narrated from *Ibni Abbas*

That the Prophet met a caravan in Rauhaa, so he asked about them. It was said that they were Muslims. They said, "And you?" He said, "[I am] the Messenger of Allah," so one lady raised a baby to him and asked, "Is there any Hajj for him?" The Prophet said, "Yes, and the reward will go to you."

When a mature minor becomes *Muhrim*, it is the duty of his or her guardian to take care of him or her. They need to make sure he or she does not make or do any *Jinayah*, and may be in his or her company when performing the *Manasik*. The guardian must give him or her the permission, as he or she could not do it without authorization. Also, the guardian will perform his two *Rakat* of *Ihram* and two *Rakat* of *Tawaf*. Finally, the minor must be clean, and his *Aurah* covered, but *wudu* (ritual cleansing) is not a must. Then whatever he or she can do himself or herself, he or she may do that, and whatever he or she cannot do, then his or her guardian may do that on his or her behalf.

Imam Tirmizi and *Ibni Maja* related a *Hadith* from *Jabir*,

> *That we performed Hajj with the Prophet. So, we said Talbiyah on behalf of children, and we did rami on their behalf as well."*

> *(This Hadith is Daeef).*

Moreover, *Ibni Umar* says,

> *"We were performing Hajj with our children. So whosoever was able to do*

rami *on their own, he did it and who could not then it was done on his behalf."*

If a mature minor commits any *Jinayah*, the custodian is responsible for them. Then the reward is for the juvenile, but there is no sin on him as he is not *Mukallaf* (bound by *Sharia*).

Imam Abu Hanifa said,

"There is no Hajj for a minor even if he is a mature one."

This could be considered religious training, like starting prayer at the age of 7. The guardian will earn the reward of training the child but as in the case of any *Jinayah* committed by the minor, there is no compensation or penalty. He says this is physical *Ibadah*, and that needs binding and if we will say that *Hajj* is permitted, then if he broke it (made it *Fasid*), he would be bound for *Qada*. However, *Imam Shafi*, *Imam Malik*, and *Imam Ahmad* said if the mature minor broke his *Hajj* with *Jima* (sexual intercourse), it is as if some adult broke his *Nafl Hajj*.

However, we say the adult is bound; having full knowledge that a given act will break the *Hajj*, while the minor is not bound.

NOTE: If a juvenile was in *Ihram* and attained puberty before *Arafat* or at *Arafat,* then his *Hajj* is considered *Fard* according to *Imam Shafi* and *Imam Ahmad*. However, *Imam Abu Hanifa* and *Imam Malik* do not consider it a *Fard Hajj*, because he must be *Mukallaf* (bound by *Islam*) at the time of *Ihram*, and in this situation the minor is not. However, *Imam Abu Hanifa* said, if he renewed his *Ihram* before *Wuquf* at *Arafat*, made the intention, said *Talbiyah* (the *Hajj* prayer), and performed *Manasik,* then his *Hajj* is *Fard*. However, if a slave did it after he was emancipated before *Wuquf* and renewed his intention and *Ihram*, etc., it cannot turn to a *Fard Hajj* because he has already started in a *Naf'l Hajj*, and he cannot break it. So, whatever he does will go in the same column as his *Naf'l Hajj*. If a minor attained the age of puberty before *Wuquf* or a slave is freed, they could put on their *Ihram* for *Hajj* now as they have not yet missed any *Wajib* in *Hajj*.

3) **NOT ENSLAVED**

As a slave does not own anything, so he has no *Istita'a*.

Nobody has the right to stop a *Muslim* from any *Ibadah* or anything that is *Wajib* for a *Muslim* to do, even parents or spouses. However, regarding *Naf'l*, a master can stop his slave, and a husband can stop his wife; they can even order them to break their *Hajj* if they have already started. However, according to *Imam Shafi'*, a husband can stop his wife from *Fard Hajj* as well, because his rights are immediate, and *Hajj* can be deferred. He cannot stop her from prayer and *Fard* fasting, but in another saying he said, he cannot stop her from *Hajj* either.

4) *ISTITA'A*

As we stated before, another fundamental pre-requisite for *Hajj* is the traveling to be out of danger, is also considered a part of *Istita'a*.

5) A woman must have her husband or another man (who is prohibited from marriage with her by law or by blood) accompany her on *Hajj*.

Then, is this condition the condition for *Nafsi - Wujub* or *Wujubi Ada*?

Ibnul Humam from *Hanafites* said,

This is for Wujubi Ada. So if she cannot perform Hajj in her lifetime, she must make a Wasiyyah [will] in this regard. However, if a woman performed Hajj without [an] Islamically required [companion], her Hajj is done, but traveling like this is a sin.

This is the *Madhab* of *Abu Hanifa*, while *Imam Malik* said,

That for Fard Hajj she could go with trustworthy colleagues: women only, or men and women both. Moreover, a lady in her mourning period after the death of her husband or after the divorce has to stay at home. However, if she went out for Hajj, then her Hajj is all right, but she has committed a sin.

According to *Imam Ahmad*, a woman divorced by *Talaq -I- Ba'in* or three divorces can go for *Hajj*. However, in the case of *Talaq -I-Raja'e* she may not go.

Imam Shafi said a woman is allowed to go for *Hajj* in the company of trustworthy women, and there should be at least three others. These are the pre-requisites of *Wujub* but with trustworthy women it is permitted for *Fard Hajj*. However, for *Naf'l*, she must have her husband or a *Muhrim* with her. To migrate from *Darul - Kufr*, she can go alone. *Ummi Salma* went out alone towards *Madinah*.

Regarding the basic concept of *Muhrim* or husband, the *Prophet* said:

> *A woman may not go on a trip for two days but with her Husband or a Muhrim (Bukhari and Muslim).*

The condition of husband or a *Muhrim* for a woman and security and safety on the way for one who is going for *Hajj* are conditions for *Wujub* according to *Hanafites* and *Shafites*. However, for *Hanbalites*, there is a similar opinion, and another one is like that of *Ibnul Humam* (a *Hanafi* jurist) that this is the condition for the performance of *Hajj*. So, someone who is bound to perform *Hajj* but cannot go because of safety concerns, or a woman who cannot go because she did not have one with whom she can go for *Hajj* may make a *Wasiyyah* in this regard.

Regarding *Istita'a*, it is also important to note that he must have enough money to meet the needs of his family until he returns, as the *Prophet* said:

> *"Enough a sin for one to lose one whom he was [supposed] to feed (Ahmad, Abu Dawud, Bayhaqi, Hakim)."*

HAJJ UL BADAL (*HAJJ* ON BEHALF OF ANOTHER)

As we mentioned before, there are three types of *Ibadat*:

I. Oral or Verbal only, like *Kalimah*

II. Physical only, like prayer and fasting

III. Financial rituals, like *Zakat*

Hajj is a combination of all three types. *Kalimah* is a declaration of *Islam* and *Iman* so everyone may declare it himself.

The physical one has a philosophy to make yourself tired by doing it, so no one can do it on behalf of another; even if the person concerned cannot do it, he will make a *Qada* of that later on. However, if he fell ill for such a time, he could have done the *Qada* of all those days of fasting, but he did not, as many days as he was in good health. Same is the case of prayer he may make *Qada*. Moreover, if he did not do that, then he may make a *Wasiyyah* for *Fidyah* (a monetary payment) to the poor. This *Fidyah* for fasting is due according to all four schools and for prayer according to *Hanafites* only. Also, if he died of the same illness without regaining sufficient health to make *Qada*, then these *Ibadat* are dropped and forgiven. However, if somebody missed these because of very old age or untreatable sickness then they may pay their *Fidyah* on their own and if not then they may make a *Wasiyyah* for *Fidyah*. The *Ibadat* which is a financial ritual like *Zakat*; one can distribute the same on behalf of the other.

CAN SOMEONE PERFORM *HAJJ* ON BEHALF OF ANOTHER?

These are the details:

The *Malikites* said there is no room for *Hajj* on behalf of someone who is still alive, as in this *Ibadah* there is the concept of physical part and practice as well. Moreover, it does not allow lieutenancy or proxy, and if someone made a *Wasiyyah* in this regard then that would be done, but it is not a well-regarded practice.

The *Hanafites* said if someone is obligated to perform, *Hajj*, but delays it until he or she is physically unable to do so, then *someone* could perform *Hajj* on his or her behalf. If the person concerned did not ask someone to perform his or her *Hajj*, then he or she must make a *Wasiyyah*. This is *Ibadah* and *Ibadah* needs *Niyat* (intention), but the dead cannot do anything with intention. So, his or her *Wasiyyah* is considered a good substitute for intention, if he or she did not make a *Wasiyyah*. But if his or her heirs did the same *Hajj* on his or her behalf, then his or her forgiveness regarding that missed *Hajj* is very much expected.

According to *Hanafites Hajj Ul Badal* is permitted in two cases:

Where the person concerned becomes unable to do *Hajj*; or if *Wasiyyah* is made.

Imams Shafi and *Ahmad* said, this type of *Hajj* is allowed in two situations:

1. One who becomes unable to perform *Hajj* due to very old age or debilitating illness or injury, but *Hajj* was feasible before. Now he or she is bound to send someone to perform *Hajj* on his or her behalf. Even though if he or she was to pay him or her, his permission is a must in this regard because this is his or her *Ibadah,* which requires intention. So, the permission is the substitute for it, or that is a gateway for the other to make intention on his behalf.

2. One who did not perform it until death was approaching him or her even though he was bound to do so. His or her heirs are bound to

arrange *Hajj* on his or her behalf even after death; the *Prophet* said:

Then the Dain [due] of Allah is much more deserving to be given [paid].

As *Imams Shafi'* and *Ahmad* said, the dues of *Allah* may be given priority over the dues of others. So, the payment may be made from the *Tarakah* (properties left behind) before the dues to the people. Shafi said it may be given priority over one's *Tajheez* and *Takfeen* expenses. Also, if someone died and did not leave any property to get his *Tajheez* or *Takfeen* expenses paid therefrom, then it is the responsibility of *Muslim* community as *Fardi Kifayah*, so if nothing remains after the payment of the dues of *Allah* the community may do that. *Imam Abu Hanifa* said in the case of death one has to make *Wasiyyah* regarding his *Hajj*, and if not, then his or her heirs, if they want, can arrange the same for him or her. However, the burial expenses must be settled before anything else. Finally, this *Wasiyyah* may be executed from one-third of the remaining property after his burial expenses and the payment of his debts.

Then according to them, a man can perform *Hajj* on behalf of another man or woman and vice versa. However, *Imam Abu Hanifa* said a man could do it on behalf of either gender. However, if a woman does the same on behalf of a man, then that is *Makrooh* (disliked). There are certain things that women cannot do in *Hajj*. It is in a different way, like *Id'tiba*, *Ramal* in *Tawaf* and running in *Sai* between the green signs. Also, she cannot shave or trim her hair.

Imam Abu Hanifa and *Imam Shafi* said, if a person becomes well after being ill, he or she is now bound to do his own *Hajj*. This is because *Hajj Ul Badal* was allowed to skip *Hajj* due to his terminal infirmity. However, he then became well enough before his death. His case is like a woman in menopause; her *Iddat* (mourning period) is on the basis of months rather than menstrual cycles, but if in the meantime her period returns, her *Iddat* period is then counted by menstrual cycles.

If someone performed the *Hajj* on behalf of a dead person without his or her *Wasiyyah* or even a request, his or her *Fard Hajj* is done. It is like a loan that is repaid by a stranger. However, *Imam Abu Hanifa* said, it is expected that by this, his or her *Fard* would be considered done.

In the case of *Wasiyyah*, as stated above, the expenses may be given from one-third of his or her remaining property after burial expenses and payment of debts, per *Imam Abu Hanifa* and *Imam Malik*. However, according to *Imam Shafi* and *Imam Ahmad*, it should be paid from his or her property before anything else. Also, in the case of *Wasiyyah*, this *Hajj* should be performed as soon as possible, while *Imam Shafi* said it could be deferred or delayed, but must be done.

Regarding *Hajj* for someone who died, *Ibni Abbas* relates,

> *That a woman from Juhainah [tribe] came to the Prophet and said, "My mother made a vow to Allah to perform Hajj, but she died before that, can I do it on her behalf?" The Prophet said, "Yes, perform Hajj on her behalf. Tell me, if there were some dues on your mother, would you have paid it? Pay the*

dues of Allah, as Allah is much more deserving of payment (Bukhari and Muslim)."

Dari Qutni narrated a *Hadith* from *Ibni Abbas*;

That a man came to the Prophet that my father died, and Hajj was due on him, should I do it on his behalf? The Prophet said, "Tell me, if your father left debts, would you have paid them on his behalf? He said yes. The Prophet replied, "So perform Hajj on behalf of your father."

The first *Hadith* is about a pledged *Hajj*, which is *Wajib* while the second one was a *Fard* one, and both cases were regarding someone who died. Also, there is another *Hadith* where there the person concerned said that his sister made a pledge of *Hajj*, but it is not mentioned there whether he was her heir or not.

Now, *Imam Malik* and *Imam Abu Hanifa* said, maybe there were the cases of *Wasiyyah*. That is why their heirs or relatives came to the

Prophet and asked about it, while *Imam Shafi* and *Imam Ahmad* said, it is not mentioned there that they had made a *Wasiyyah*. However, their relatives were of the view that the *Hajj* was due on them, which is why they asked the *Prophet*. However, regarding one who is still alive, there are *Ahadith* as well:

Ibni Abbas and others said that a woman from *Khath'am* (a tribe) said to the *Prophet*,

> *"Indeed, Hajj became due on my father when he was very old, he cannot stay on the back of a camel."*

The Prophet said,

> *"Then perform Hajj on his behalf."*

Ibni Abbas said;

> *The Prophet heard a man saying, "Labbaik from Shubrumah." He asked him, "Who is Shubrumah?" The man said, "My brother or my relative." The Prophet said, "Make this one from yourself, then do another one from Shubrumah" (Bukhari, Muslim, Abu Dawud, Tirmizi, Nisa'i, Ibni Maja).*

The first *Hadith* clearly mentioned that the man was still alive and the *Prophet* ordered his daughter for *Hajj Ul Badal*, while the second hadith did not mention whether *Shubrumah* was alive or not. *Imam Abu Hanifa, Imam Shafi* and *Imam Ahmad* allowed the same from someone still alive. However, *Imam Malik* said, there is no *Hajj* on behalf of someone still living.

We say that what the three *Imams* said that is reasonable as the financial side of *Ibadah* is more obvious in *Hajj*, and that type of *Ibadah* accommodates proxies.

THE CONDITIONS FOR *HAJJ UL BADAL*

There are a few conditions that all schools have agreed upon. There are some other conditions where their opinions differ:

I. The person concerned becomes physically unable to do it on his own. This is agreed upon by *Imam Abu Hanifa, Imam Shafi* and *Imam Ahmad*, while *Imam Malik* said,

    "There is no Hajj Ul Badal from one who is alive."

    They all agreed that it was valid for someone who is dead. However, according to *Abu Hanifa* and *Malik* if he has made a *Wasiyyah*, while *Shafi* and *Ahmad* say even without *Wasiyyah*.

II. The person's inability may be of such a nature that it continues until death. So, if someone did his *Hajj*, and then he or she recovers, now he or she must do his *Hajj* again. This is according to *Imam Abu Hanifa* and *Imam Shafi*, while *Imam Ahmad* said, that first *Hajj*, i.e., *Hajj Ul Badal* was his *Fard Hajj*, and it is done.

III. The expenses must be given by him, in total or nearly, according to *Hanafites*. If the heir did the same by his money but on behalf of the deceased, if he had not made the *Wasiyyah*, that would be considered his *Fard Hajj*. If he or she had made the *Wasiyyah* from the property he or she is leaving behind, and the heir paid for it from his own property or money, then that is not considered a *Hajj* of the deceased because, due to his *Wasiyyah* the expenses were specifically from the property of the deceased. However, according to *Imam Shafi* and *Imam Ahmad*, whosoever performed *Hajj* on behalf of the deceased, it does not matter if he made a *Wasiyyah* or not, or even in case of his *Wasiyyah* the heir did it from his own money, that is all right.

IV. The *Na'ib* (proxy) who performs *Hajj* on behalf of someone may make intention from that person, according to all schools.

V. The lieutenant may make the *Ihram* from *Meeqat* as the person asked for. If he has asked him for *Ifrad*, but he did *Tamattu* then that is his own *Hajj*. He is responsible for his *Hajj* according to *Hanafites*, and if he did *Qiran*, then he is responsible for the expenses according to *Abu Hanifa*. While this is allowed according to *Abu Yusuf* and *Muhammad* based upon *Istihsan* (preference), this is the opinion of *Imam Shafi* and *Imam Ahmad* as well. Moreover, if he asked him for *Hajj*, but he did *Umrah* then he went out to *Meeqat* and put on *ihram* for *Hajj*, then he is not responsible for anything, according to *Imam Shafi'* and *Imam Ahmad*. If he ordered him for *Tamattu*, but he did *Qiran*, that is also permitted according to *Shafi* and *Ahmad* without any responsibility, and in this case if he did *Ifrad* then that is from the original person. However, he will give him back the expenses of *Umrah*, and if the order was for *Qiran* and he did *Ifrad* or *Tamattu*, then that is from the original person. However, he will return whatever he has not spent. If he mentioned the place where from his *Hajj* may be done and mentioned the money, then his words may be honored. However, if he has not mentioned anything, then it must be from his city.

According to *Imam Shafi*, the *Hajj* must be from the *Meeqat* of that person. According to *Imam Ahmad*, it must be from the town of that person and if the one-third of *Tarakah* falling short if he is going to do his *Hajj* from his *Meeqat* or his *"city."* Then his Hajj should be done from a place that money can afford it. This is according to *Hanafites*.

VI. The person concerned must have asked someone for the purpose if he wants his *Hajj* to be done from him in his lifetime, according to *Abu Hanifa, Shafi'* and *Ahmad*.

VII. The person who is going to perform *Hajj* on behalf of someone else may not charge any wages for that, as this is *Ibadah*. According to *Abu Hanifa*, no wages are allowed for *Ibadat* as *Ibni Maja* related a *Hadith* from *Ubai Ibni Ka'b*. He was teaching *Qur'an* to someone, so he gifted him a bow, so *Ubai* asked the *Prophet* about it.

The *Prophet* said to him:

> *If it makes you happy to necklace a bow of fire, then necklace it.*

However, according to *Jumhur* as well as the latest *Hanafites* scholars, it is permitted to take some compensation for some *Ibadat*. Otherwise, some *Ibadat* could not be practiced, like the teaching of *Quran* and *Sunnah* or even an *Imamat*. The *Prophet* said, when *Sahabah* asked him about those 30 lambs they received as compensation when *Abu Saeed Al Khudri* did *Ruqya* to one of them who was bitten by a poisonous insect:

> *The much more deserving thing you have taken compensation for, that is the book of Allah (Bukhari).*

We say the compensation for *Ibadat* may be without proposal and acceptance, i.e., without a contract, so it should be considered reciprocation. Alternatively, if a contract is made, then it should be for his confinement and having his time reserved for him or them. That is why those who do not allow this say that the *Hajj* must be from the original person who asked for it. However, as the *Ijarah* is voidable, the one who is doing the *Hajj* is eligible for payment for his needs and necessities. However, any unspent extra may be returned to the original person. If he or his heirs allow it, it may be made a gift. However, if he committed any *Jinayah* in *Hajj*, then he has to pay, and if he broke his *Hajj* he will make the *Qada* and return all the money to the original person or his heirs, and the *Hajj* will be that of the doer.

According to *Imam Malik* in a case where *Hajj Ul Badal* is allowed, it is wrong to take compensation for that or any other *Ibadah* except teaching of *Qur'an* and *Sunnah*.

If the contract was for a specific amount, then it is the responsibility of the proxy to accomplish the job with those funds. If he or she saves any money, that is his or hers to keep. However, if he or she falls short of money, then he or she must spend his or her own to cover the shortfall. However, if no amount was fixed and he or she falls short of money, he or she may ask for more, and if he or she saved any, it must be returned.

Also, the rules for hiring in general must be taken into consideration for the *Hajj*.

VIII. The person who is going to do *Hajj* on behalf of another must be a *Mukallaf* according to all. However, *Imam Abu Hanifa* said a mature minor is also eligible.

IX. This is a must for one who is doing the *Hajj* of someone else that he has done his own already. This is according to *Imam Shafi'* and *Imam Ahmad*, as this is mentioned in the *hadith* where the *Prophet* told the person that do your own first, and then another one from *Shubrumah*. Also, *Abu Dawud* related a *Hadith*:

There is no Saroorah in Islam.

Saroorah is a *Hajj* from someone when the doer has not done his or her own before. *Imam Abu Hanifa* and *Imam Malik* allow it, but is *Makrooh* as the *Prophet* never asked the lady of *Khath'am* whether she had performed her own before or not. It is the case in the case of the woman from *Juhainah* and the *Hadith* of *Dari Qutni*.

X. If he has mentioned one person by name to perform his *Hajj*, then that person is must to do it. However, if he has given him the authority to do what he sees suitable, then he can appoint another one to perform his *Hajj*.

XI. The proxy may not break his or her *Hajj*, and if he or she does, then even though if he or she did its *Qada* it is not for the original person. He or she may pay him or her whatever he or she has spent according to *Hanafites*.

XII. He or she must make only one intention for *Hajj* on behalf of that person. If he or she falls ill, he should be in *Ihram* till his recovery according to *Jumhur*. While, according to *Hanafites*, he can get out of *Ihram* if he cannot do anything, and the doctors also advise rest.

MAWAQEET

This is the plural of *Meeqat,* which means a specific time or a particular place.

Regarding time,

Allah said:

They ask you about crescents [the moon]. Tell them these are Mawaqeet for people and Hajj (2:189).

The Hajj is [has] known months [prescribed] (2:197).

Shawwal, Zul Qadah and *Zul Hijjah* as a whole are the months of *Hajj,* as *Allah* used the plural word *Ash'hur.* Also, *Allah* used a plural proverb after this and said *Feehinna.* These three are mentioned by *Umar, Abdullah Ibni Umar,* and *Abdullah Ibni Abbas.*

So, to *Malikites,* the time of *Ihram* for *Hajj* starts from the night of *Eid Ul Fitr* until the break of dawn of *Eid Ul Udha.* So, whoever did *Ihram* for *Hajj* before this dawn, and he was in *Arafat,* so he found the time to do *Hajj,* according to

Malikites, the *Ruk'n* is to stay at *Arafat* at night. *Ihram* for *Hajj* before *Shawal* is *Makrooh* as it is allowable to put on your *Ihram* before *Meeqat* (the specific place as *Meeqat* (place and time) is required for *Hajj* is to be perfect not for its *Wujub*, so according to them, *Tawaf Ul Ifadah* is permissible until the end of *Zul Hijjah*.

It is best for the people of *Makkah* to put on *Ihram starting* from the first of *Zul Hijjah*. According to *Hanafites* and *Hanbalites*, the months of *Hajj* are *Shawwal*, *Zul Qadah*, and the 10 days of *Zul Hijjah*. As it is said by *Ibni Masud, Ibni Abbas, Ibni Umar, Ibni Zubair* and *Abu Dawud* narrated a *Hadith* that:

The day of the great Hajj is the day of "Nah'r" [sacrifice].

Imam Bukhari narrates that the *Prophet* said in his *Khutbah* (sermon) on *Yaumun Nah'r*:

This is the day of the great Hajj.

Moreover, on *Yaumun Nah'r* the *Fard Tawaf* is taking place, also the *Rami*, the sacrifice, the shave or trim, and *Sai* and return to *Mina*. The *Hajj* is missed if one cannot do it until the end of the tenth. So, the *Ayah* means the two months and ten days of the third one. So, if someone put on his *ihram* before these months for *Hajj*, it does not convert to *Umrah*. However, the *Manasik* of *Hajj* may be done in its time only as *Ihram* is a pre-requisite for *Hajj* and *Umrah*. However, he put it on before time is like someone made *Wudu* for *Zuhr* before its time. To them, this *Meeqat* of time is like the *Meeqat* of place, but still to put on *Ihram* for *Hajj* before these months is *Makrooh,* as *Ibni Abbas* said:

> *This is Sunnah not to put on ihram for Hajj but in the months of Hajj.*

Shafites and *Hanbalites* said that these months are *Shawwal*, *Zul Qadah* and ten days of *Zul Hijjah* till dawn break of *Yaumun Nah'r*. However, if someone put on his *Ihram* for *Hajj* before *Shawwal*, his *Ihram* turns to *Umrah* as that is before the proper time. So, it will turn to a similar *Ibadah*, which for the time is not unique, like if someone started *Zuhr* prayer before the time, it would turn to *Naf'l*. So, they say the *Meeqat* of time is like the time of prayer. Thus, in one year there is only one *Hajj*.

MEEQAT (THE APPOINTED PLACE)

Mawaqeet are the appointed places outside *Makkah* at which every *Muslim* is bound to put on *Ihram* for *Umrah* and for *Hajj*, as it is not allowed to pass over these places without *Ihram*. If someone does pass through while not wearing *Ihram* they have to make *Dum* (sacrifice). It is permitted to put on *Ihram* before *Meeqat* according to all schools, and that is best according to *Hanafites*. For those who are at *Makkah* even though they are from somewhere else, the *Meeqat* for *Hajj* is *Makkah* as the *Prophet* ordered his *Sahabah* to do so. For those who are living inside the limits of *Haram*, their *Meeqat* is their house. However to some scholars if one made intention from *Meeqat* but did not put on his *Ihram*, and put it on after passing the *Meeqat* but before doing of any ritual, then there is no *"Dom"* on him. This *Fatwa* could be given in circumstances.

It is recommended if someone can do it from *Masjid Al Haram* if possible. However, his or her

Meeqat for *Umrah* is the nearest part of *Hil* (the area in between *Mawaqeet* and limits of *Haram)*. This is because *Hajj* is *Arafah* and that is situated in the *Hil* area, while *Umrah* is done in *Haram* in such a way that in both there will be some traveling. Also, he will get together in both the *Hil* and the *Haram* as that is a condition of each *Ihram*. So, if someone put on his or her *Ihram* for *Umrah* inside the limits of *Haram*, he or she must make a sacrifice, but if he or she went to *Hil* after his *Ihram* before doing the *Umrah*, then his *Dum* is dropped.

The best place in *Hil* for *Umrah* according to *Shafites* is *Ji'irranah*. As the *Prophet* performed *Umrah* there as narrated by *Imam Bukhari* and *Imam Muslim*, then *Tan'eem,* as the *Prophet* ordered *Aisha* to do it there. Next is *Hudaibiyah*, while the best one according to *Hanafites* and *Hanbalites* is *Tan'eem*. As that is the closest part of *Hil*, then *Ji'irranah*, then *Hudaibiyah* and according to *Malikites* that is optional to do it from *Tan'eem* or *Ji'irranah*.

For people of the *Hil* area, the *Meeqat* for *Umrah* and *Hajj* both according to *Malikites* is their house, if that is close to *Makkah*, then *Meeqat*.

According to *Shafites* and *Hanbalites*, whoever is going on a way not passing right over *Meeqat*, may put on his *Ihram* from such a place that is in line with *Meeqat*. If there were two *Meeqat* in line to that place, then he or she may put on *Ihram* in line with the *Meeqat* that is closer to him or her; if both the *Meeqats* were equidistant to him or her, then he may put on *Ihram* in line with the one that is farther from *Makkah*. For those whose house is in between *Meeqat* and *Makkah*, his *Meeqat* is his house.

Note: For anyone who passes over *Meeqat* without *Ihram* because he or she was not planning to perform *Hajj* or *Umrah*, his or her *Meeqat* is the place he or she is therein.

According to *Hanafites*, the *Meeqat* for the people of the *Hil* area, for both *Hajj* and *Umrah* is their place/village. Or even any place from the *Hil* area in between their village and the limits of *Haram*. This is what *Ali* and *Ibni Masud* said. Also, according to *Hanafites* it is allowed for people in *Hil* to enter *Makkah* without *Ihram* if they are going there for some other reason.

There are five *Mawaqeet* for outsiders, those who are coming from areas outside (*Mawaqeet*) with the intention of performing *Hajj* or *Umrah*, as *Ibni Abbas* narrated that the *Prophet* appointed for people of *Madinah*, *Zul Hulaifa*; for the people of *Sham*, *Juhfah*; for people of *Najd*, *Qarnal Manazil*; and for people of *Yemen, Yalamlam*; and the *Prophet* said:

> *These places are for them, and those who are passing through these locations, and they are not from these sites for anyone intending Hajj and Umrah. Also, whoever is inside these places then their appointed place for ihram is their village and so is the case that people of Makkah, as they will put on Ihram from Makkah.*

The fifth one is *Zat-Irq*, as *Imam Muslim* narrated from *Jabir*:

And, the Ihram place of the people of Iraq is Zat-Irq.

1. *Zul Hulaifa* – It is outside *Madinah* towards *Makkah* that is called *Aabari Ali* also. This is the farthest *Meeqat*.

2. *Juhfah* – This is also known as *Rabigh*.

3. *Zat-Irq* – This is a village to the northeast of *Makkah*.

4. *Yalamlam* – A mountain to the south of *Makkah*.

5. *Qarnal Manazil* – This is also called *Qarnuth Tha'aalib*.

For anyone who passes over any *Meeqat* without *Ihram*, if he or she returns to *Meeqat* and puts on *Ihram* there, then there is no *Dum* required. And if he or she crosses over *Meeqat* and puts on *ihram* after that, but he or she has still not done any of the *Manasik*, then *Imam Abu Hanifa* said, if he returns to *Meeqat* and said *Talbiyah*, then there is no *Dum* required, as *Ibni Abbas* said to one who passed over *Meeqat* without *Ihram*:

Go back to Meeqat and say Talbiyah, otherwise there is no Hajj for you.

The *Shafites*, *Hanbalites*, *Abu Yusuf* and *Muhammad* said that if before performing of any of the *Manasik*, a person crosses over *Meeqat* and put on *Ihram* and then returns to *Meeqat,* there is no *Dum* on him, whether he or she says *Talbiyah* or not. However, all of them said as long as he or she has not done any of the *Manasik* he or she must return to the *Meeqat*. But *Malikites* said *Dum* is required even if he returns to *Meeqat* and said *Talbiyah*.

Also, we said, the *Meeqat* for *Hajj* for someone in *Makkah* is *Makkah* and for *Umrah* the closest part of *Hil*, but if he or she does not go to *Hil* to put on *Ihram* for *Umrah*, he or she must make a *Dum*; but if he or she goes to *Hil* after putting on *Ihram*, then the *Dum* is dropped.

If someone passes over *Meeqat* without *Ihram*, he or she must go back to *Meeqat* and put on *Ihram*. However, if he or she does not do so for some reason, then he or she must make a *Dum*.

One who puts on *Ihram* after *Meeqat* is considered to have broken his or her *Hajj*, and so the *Dum* is not dropped according to *Shafites* and

Hanbalites; while according to *Hanafites*, *Dum* is dropped because he or she has to make a *Qada* of that *Hajj* anyway.

Ihram is better if one puts it on from his or her place if it was during the month of *Hajj* according to *Hanafites*. *Ali* and *Ibni Masud* said the perfectness of *Hajj* and *Umrah* is to put on *Ihram* from your place.

Also, *Prophet Muhammad* said:

> *Whoever put on ihram for Hajj or Umrah from Masjid Ul Aqsa to Masjid Ul Haram, his sins are forgiven or Jannah is due for him, and Umar put on his ihram from Al Quds. Umar said to Dabbi Ibni Mabad, who put on ihram from his house: You have been guided to the Sunnah of your Prophet (Abu Dawud).*

Jumhur said, *Ihram* from *Meeqat* is better, as the *Prophet* and his *Sahabah* did it there from, and the *Prophet* did it from *Zul Hulaifa* for *Hajj* and also in *Umrat Ul Hudaibiyah*.

Also, that is the easy way, as *Ihram* has a lot of restrictions.

The *Prophet* said:

One of you may enjoy his position without Ihram as much as he can, as he does not know what will happen to him in his Ihram (Abu Yala).

Hassan says that *Imran Ibni Husain* put on his *ihram* in his city and the news reached *Umar*. So, *Umar* became angry and said,

"People will hear from one another that a man from the companions of the Prophet put on his ihram *in his city, and he said that Abdullah Ibni Aamir put on his Ihram in Khorasan, so when he came to him, he disliked it (Saeed Ibni Mansoor and Ath'ram)."*

Imam Bukhari also narrated that *Uthman* disliked the donning of *Ihram* from *Khorasan* and *Kirman*. We also prefer this practice to put on *Ihram* and make *Niyat* from *Meeqat*. And the contradiction in the reaction of *Umar* that in case of *Ibni Mabad* he appreciated that he put on *Ihram* from his house and disliked that in case of *Ibni Aamir* means that *Ibni Mabad* had put on his

Ihram only and not made his intention their from, but from *Meeqat* while *Ibni Aamir* had made his intention from his home also and restrictions came with intention. Or The *Hadith* regarding *Bait Ul Maqdas* is *Daeef*. What *Umar* said to *Dabbi* was regarding *Qiran* that you have been guided towards *Sunnah*, the saying of *Umar* and *Ali* that

> *"Perfectness of Umrah is to start is from your village"*

Means to start traveling for it as *Sufyan* and *Ahmad* explained it in this way. We can say, put on *Ihram* from your place and make the intention and say *Talbiyah* from *Meeqat*.

What are the responsibilities for someone who completed *Hajj* or *Umrah* and entered *Makkah*, passing over *Meeqat*, or a *Makki* who was traveling?

Anyone who is coming from outside the *Meeqat* area, so if his entering to *Makkah* is not a repeated case, then *Shafites* said he should put on *Ihram* and perform *Umrah*, and it is *Makrooh* to enter there without *Ihram*, *Imam Malik* and *Imam*

Ahmad said this is required to put on *Ihram* while *Imam Abu Hanifa* said, if his residence is in a *Meeqat* area means he is not passing over *Meeqat* or close to *Makkah*, he can enter without *Ihram*. Moreover, those who are going out and coming back again and again, like drivers, may enter without *Ihram*, as in the *Hadith* of *Ibni Abbas*, this is mentioned for those who used to go to cut and collect firewood, and those who are living in *Haram* area.

Entering inside the limits of *Haram* is like entering *Makkah*. Moreover, if *Ihram* is required when someone is entering *Makkah* but he or she does not put it on, there is no *Qada* on them, but he or she has committed a sin. This is according to *Shafites*, but a *Qada* is a must for such a person according to *Abu Hanifa*. However, if someone was entering *Makkah* to fight the rebellions, for example, then there is no requirement of *Ihram* on them. This is because the *Prophet* at the time of the conquest entered without *Ihram* as *Imam Muslim* and *Nisa'i* narrated from *Jabir*.

NOTE: As we mentioned before, a non-Muslim is not bound by the rules of *Sharia*, i.e., *Ibadat*.

A minor is also not bound, and a slave is not bound to perform *Hajj*. So, if one of these groups is inside the *Meeqat* areas, such as *Hil*, and the non-*Muslim* accepts *Islam*, the minor attains the age of majority, or the slave becomes emancipated, then according to *Malikites* and *Hanbalites*, they will don their *Ihram* from the place they are without binding for a *Jenayat* of *Dum*, as they are considered as *Makki* or one in *Hil*. But according to *Shafites*, they are bound to make *Dum*, and according to *Abu Hanifa*, the slave is bound to give *Dum* as *Nafsi Wujub* was there on him or her.

UMRAH (AL HAJJ UL ASGHAR)

Umrah is known as the minor *Hajj* or *Al Hajj Ul Asghar*, while *Hajj* is called *Al Hajj Ul Akbar*. *Imam Bukhari* and others narrated from *Aisha* and *Ibni Umar* that the *Prophet* performed four *Umrah*. Also, *Imam Bukhari, Imam Muslim* and *Imam Ahmad* from *Anas* narrate the same number as well, and these are:

i. *Umrat Ul Hudaibiyah* in the 6th year.

ii. *Umrat Ul Qada*, the following year, the 7th

iii. *Umrah* from *Ji'irranah* where he distributed the spoils of *Hunain* in the 8th year.

iv. *Umrah* with his *Hajj* in the 9th year. The aforementioned three were in the month of *Zul Qadah*.

THE CONTENTS OF *UMRAH*

According to *Hanafites Umrah* has only one *Ruk'n*. And that is *Tawaf*, while *Ihram* is *Shart* and *Sai* and the ritual shave/trim are *Wajib* but not *Arkan*. According to *Malikites* and *Hanbalites*, the *Arkan* of *Umrah* are:

i. *Ihram*

ii. *Tawaf*

iii. *Sai*, while according to *Shafites* the shave/trim is a fourth *Ruk'n*.

Umrah is *Sunnah Muakkadah* according to *Hanafites* and *Malikites* and *Fard* at ease according to *Shafites*, and *Fard* the sooner according to *Hanbalites*.

The *Arkan* of *Hajj* are, according to *Hanafites*:

i. *Wuquf* at *Arafat*

ii. *Tawaf Ul Ifadah*

Moreover, according to *Malikites Arkan* of *Hajj* are:

i. *Ihram*

ii. *Wuquf* at *Arafah*.

iii. *Tawaf Ul Ifadah*, and

iv. *Sai* while to *Imam Shafi* a 5Th one is shave/trim.

As we said before, *Umrah* is *Fard* according to *Ahmad Ibni Hanbal*, the sooner one can do like *Hajj*. That is *Fard* but on ease of the person like *Hajj* according to *Shafi'* and that is *Sunnah* according to *Malik* and *Abu Hanifa*.

There is no specific time for *Umrah*, as it is allowed all year long. But that is *Makrooh* on *Arafah* day, on *Nah'r* day and in *Ayyamut Tashreeq* 11Th, 12th and 13th of *Zul Hijjah* according to *Abu Hanifa*. That is prohibited for one in *Hajj* as long as something from *Manasik* is still due on him, like *Rami*, and that is allowed any day according to *Malik* and *Ahmad*.

To do more than one *Umrah* in one year is allowed according to *Jumhur*. *Imam Malik* said, in one year more than one *Umrah* is *Makrooh*. He said this even though *Umrah* is allowed at any time of the year. But a *Haji* cannot do it if he or she has not done all the *Manasik* of *Hajj*. So, if a

Haji stayed in *Mina* for 13Th of *Zul Hijjah*, he cannot put on *Ihram* for *Umrah*, as long as he has not completed the *Rami* and if he has left *Mina* on 12Th of *Zul Hijjah*, still he cannot put on *Ihram* for *Umrah* until an estimated time of *Rami* is passed after *Zawal* (declination of the sun to the west). But *Ihram* for that is still *Makrooh* after he did *Rami* on 13th, but the sun has not set. If he put on *Ihram* after *Rami* on the 13th before sunset, he must delay his *Tawaf* and *Sai* till sunset. If he did it before sunset it is void; he must do it again after sunset, otherwise he would be considered in *Ihram*.

ISSUES COMPONENTIZED

1. *NIYYAT* or Intention	*SHART* (Pre-requisite) according to *Hanafites*	*RUKN* or Constituent according to *Jumhur*
2. *IHRAM* from *Meeqat*.	< *WAJIB* ACCORDING TO ALL FOUR SCHOOLS OF JURISPRUDENCE >	
3. *TALBIYAH* after *Ihram* and also as much as one can.	*WAJIB* according to *Hanafites* and *Malikites*	*SUNNAH* according to *Shafites* and *Hanbalites*
4. *GHUSL* or shower for *Ihram*.	< *SUNNAH* ACCORDING TO ALL AND SAME IS THE CASE OF PERFUME BEFORE *IHRAM* >	
5. INTENTION for *Tawaf*.	*SHART* according to *Hanafites*	*WAJIB* according to	*SUNNAH* according to

84

		Mal-ikites	*Shafites* and *Han-balites*
6. STARTING *Tawaf* from *Hajar -I- Aswad*	*WAJIB* according to *Hanafites* and *Malikites*	*SHART* according to *Shafites* and *Hanbalites*	
7. To have the *Kaaba* to his LEFT shoulder when making *Tawaf*.	*WAJIB* according to *Hanafites*	*SHART* according to *Jumhur*.	
8. To do *Tawaf* WALKING for those who are able to do it.	*WAJIB* according to *Hanafites* and *Malikites*	*SUNNAH* according to *Shafites* and *Hanbalites*	
9. To be with *WUDU* when making *Tawaf*.	*WAJIB* according to *Hanafites*	*SHART* according to *Jumhur*	

10. CLEANLINESS of body, dress and place.	*SUNNAH* according to *Hanafites*	*SHART* according to *Jumhur*
11. *Tawaf* OUTSIDE *Hateem*	*WAJIB* according to *Hanafites*	*SHART* according to *Jumhur*
12. *Tawaf* to be IN the *Masjid*	< *SHART* ACCORDING TO ALL >	
13. *Tawaf* to be SEVEN rounds	4 rounds are *Fard* and the remaining 3 are *WAJIB* according to *Hanafites*	*SHART* according to *Jumhur*
14. The rounds of *Tawaf* should be CONSTANT without any interval in between.	*SUNNAH* according to *Hanafites* and *Shafites*	*WAJIB* according to *Malikites* and *Hanbalites*

15. To cover the *AURAH* in *Tawaf*	*WAJIB* according to *Hanafites*	*SHART* according to *Jumhur*
16. TWO *Rakat* after *Tawaf*	*WAJIB* according to *Hanafites* and *Malikites*	*SUNNAH* according to *Shafites* and *Hanbalites*
17. *TAWAF* of *Umrah*	< *RUKN* or Constituent according to all schools >	
18. *Sai* in BETWEEN *Safa'* and *Marwah*	*WAJIB* according to *Hanafites*	*RUKN* or Constituent according to *Jumhur*
19. *Sai* to be AFTER *Tawaf*	*WAJIB* according to *Hanafites* and *Malikites*	*SHART* according to *Shafites* and *Hanbalites*
20. INTENTION for *Sai*	*WAJIB* according to *Hanafites*	*SHART* according to *Jumhur*
21. To START *Sai* at *Safa* and	*WAJIB* according to *Hanafites*	*SHART* according to *Jumhur*

to finish at *Marwah*		
22. To do *Sai* by WALK one who can do it.	*WAJIB* according to *Hanafites* and *Malikites*	*SUNNAH* according to *Shafites* and *Hanbalites*
23. *Sai* to be of SEVEN rounds.	4 Rounds are *WAJIB* according to *Hanafites*, and the remaining 3 are *Sunnah*	*SHART* according to *Jumhur*
24. The rounds of *Sai* should be CONSTANT without any interval in between	*SUNNAH* according to *Hanafites* and *Shafites*	*SHART* according to *Malikites* and *Hanbalites*

25. SHAVING or TRIMMING the head for men, and cutting hair about 1/3 of a finger length for women.	*WAJIB* according to *Jumhur*	*FARD* according to *Shafites*, while one saying of theirs is like that of *Jumhur*
26. *Umrah* in *AYYAMUT TASHREEQ*	*MAKROOH TAHREEMI* according to *Hanafites,* while there is no room for *Umrah* in these days according to *Malikites* and to do it after *Rami* on 13th of *Zul Hijjah*	That is ok according to *Hanbalites* and ok according to *Shafites*, but after that one is considered to have finished his or her *Hajj*.

	before sunset is *Makrooh*.	

HAJJ

Regarding *Hajj,* the best type of *Hajj* is *Qiran* according to *Hanafites* as the *Prophet* said:

Make Ihram, O family of Muhammad, for Umrah in Hajj (Tahawi).

According to *Hanbalites* and *Shafites*, *Hajj-I-Ifrad* is the best if one has done already an *Umrah* in that year. They say that the *Prophet* did *Hajj-I-Ifrad*. *Imam Bukhari* and *Imam Muslim* relate from *Aisha* that the *Prophet* did *Ihram* for *Hajj*. *Qiran* is the best, according to *Hanafites* and *Tamattu* according to *Malikites*. The *Hanbalites* said in one saying that *Tamattu* is the best type of *Hajj*, then *Ifrad* and then *Qiran*.

They referred to the *Ahadith* regarding *Hajj* of the *Prophet* as *Anas* said regarding *Qiran* and the *Hadith* of *Aisha*, narrated by *Imam Bukhari* and *Imam Muslim*, she said the *Prophet* did *Ihram* for *Hajj* (*Ifrad*) and *Ibni Umar* said; the *Prophet* did *Tamattu*.

In *Hajj-I-Ifrad* one may take a shower and put on some fragrance for *Ihram* according to

Jumhur. But no fragrances according to *Malikites*, so one has to put on *Ihram*, pray two *Rakat* for *Ihram*, makes intention for *Hajj* only from *Meeqat* and says *Talbiyah*. This is *Hajj-I-Ifrad*.

When one arrives in *Makkah* one will make *Tawaf-I-Qudum*, which is *Sunnah* according to *Jumhur*, and *Wajib* according to *Imam Malik*. If he or she wants to make a *Sai* after this *Tawaf*, then there is no *Sai* due on him after *Tawaf Ul Ifadah*. He will be in *Ihram* until he shaves on the 10th of *Zul Hijjah*.

So on the 8th of *Zul Hijjah*, he or she will stay the night at *Mina*. On the 9th of *Zul Hijjah*, he or she will go to *Arafat* to stay there until after sunset. After sunset, he or she will go to *Muzdalafah*. He will perform the *Maghreb* and *Isha* prayers there at *Muzdalafah* and will stay the night there. On 10Th of *Zul Hijjah* after sunrise, he will leave for *Mina*. Then he will go to *Jamarat Ul Aqabah*, the closest one to *Makkah*. He or she will do *Rami* with seven pebbles, and then if he or she wants to slaughter, as this is *Sunnah* in *Hajji Ifrad*, he will do that. After that, he or she will shave/trim, take a shower, and take off the *Ihram*.

It is best to go to *Haram* to make *Tawaf Ul Ifadah* on 10th. But if he or she has not done the *Sai* after *Tawaf Ul Qudum,* then he or she will do that as well.

After this, he or she will go back to *Mina* and stay the night on the 11th of *Zul Hijjah*. He or she will do all three *Jamarat*, the *Sughra*, the *Wasta* and then the *Kubra* (*Aqabah*), each with seven pebbles after *Zawal*, then go back to *Mina* and stay the night. Then on the 12th of *Zul Hijjah*, he or she will do these three *Jamarat* the same way as the day before, and will do that after *Zawal*. Now he or she has the option to stay for another day and night at *Mina* and do the same practice on the 13th as well. However, on the 13th it is allowed according to Hanafites before *Zawal*, but not according to *Jumhur*. Alternatively, if he or she wants, he or she can go from *Mina* after *Rami* on the 12th. All the requirements of the *Hajj* are fulfilled now, but if he or she is an outsider then one *Tawaf* is remaining, and that is *Tawaf Ul Wida* or *Tawaf Us Sadr*.

HAJJI TAMATTU

In this type of *Hajj*, one will do the same practice at *Meeqat*. However, one's intention will be for *Umrah* only, so when one arrives at *Makkah* he or she will perform *Umrah*, and will thus become totally *Halal*. Then on the 8th of *Zul Hijjah*, he or she will put on his *ihram* at the place where he or she is staying. This *Ihram* is for *Hajj*; then the whole procedure is as we have mentioned in *Hajji Ifrad*.

However, the *Qurbani* (sacrifice) here is *Wajib*.

HAJJI QIRAN

First we have to know once again that *Hajj* is of three types:

i. *HAJJ-I-IFRAD:*

Where someone has to make *Niyat* for *Hajj* alone when passing by *Meeqat*, then he or she will be in *Ihram* until throwing the pebbles at *Jamarat Ul Aqabah* and on shave/trim. Woman can cut her hair because there is no *Wajib Qurbani* in this type of *Hajj*, but that is *Sunnah,* so to shave the hair or cut it after the *Qurbani* if he/she is doing that, is also *Sunnah*.

ii. *HAJJI TAMATTU:*

When someone is going for *Hajj* but he or she put on *Ihram* for *Umrah* alone when passing by the *Meeqat*. He or she performs his *Umrah* as per the details already discussed. Then on the 8th of *Zul Hijjah*, he or she will put on *Ihram* for the *Hajj* and perform it as per details we will discuss later.

iii. *HAJJI QIRAN:*

In this type of *Hajj*, one may put on *Ihram* and make intention for *Hajj* and *Umrah*, both from *Meeqat* and when he arrives at *Makkah*. According to all and then after that according to *Hanafites*, he or she will make *Tawaf I Qudum* also, and will remain in *ihram* just like one in *Hajji Ifrad* from the 8th of *Zul Hijjah*. He or she will adopt the same procedures of *Hajj* as we outlined in *Hajji Ifrad*. However, here also, like *Tamattu*, the *Qurbani* (slaughter) is *Wajib*.

All that we wrote for *Umrah* apply to *Hajj* in the same way. Here we will give a sketch of other *Aamal*, which are unique to *Hajj*.

When someone puts on *Ihram* and makes the intention of *Hajj* and *Umrah* simultaneously when passing by *Meeqat*. He or she will perform his or her *Umrah* without shave or trim or taking off *Ihram*. He or she will perform his *Hajj* as well, as per details we will discuss later.

All these rules and their status that we will describe apply in all three types of *Hajj*, but there are slight differences in a few things. In *Hajj-I-Qiran*, one will put on *Ihram* at the *Meeqat* and make intention for both *Hajj* and *Umrah*. Then he or she will perform *Umrah* without a shave/trim and without taking off the *Ihram*. He or she will perform *Tawaf Ul Qudum* also according to *Hanafites*, while to *Jumhur* he or she should make the intention for *Tawaf Ul Qudum* with the same *Tawaf* of *Umrah*. So that can be two in one and according to *Hanafites* if he makes another *Sai* after *Tawaf Ul Qudum*. Then there is no need of another *Sai* after *Tawaf Ul Ifadah*. However, in *Hajj-I-Tamattu* one has to put on *Ihram* on the 8th of *Zul Hijjah* from *Makkah* where he or she is staying or from *Masjid Ul Haram*. In *Hajj-I-Tamattu* and *Hajj-I-Qiran*, *Zab'h / Qurbani* is *Wajib*.

SKETCH FOR *HAJJI-IFRAD*

1. *NIYYAT* for *Hajj*.	*SHART* according to *Hanafites*.	*RUKN* according to *Jumhur*
2. To put on *IHRAM* from *Meeqat*	< *WAJIB* according to all schools >	
3. *TAWAF-I-QUDUM*	< *SUNNAH* according to all schools > But the *Madhab* of *Malikites* is that this is *Wajib*	
NOTE: Then all details we have given in the *Umrah* are meant here as well, but if he did *Sai* with *Tawaf Ul Qudum* then there is no *Sai* after *Tawaf Ul Ifadah*		
4. To stay at *MINIA* the night of *Arafat*	< *SUNNAH* according to all schools >	

5. *WUQUF*'s time at *Arafat*	< From after *ZAWAL* time until dawn break of the 10th of *Zul Hijjah* according to all schools >	
6. To stay until after sunset at *Arafat* if he has started it at day-time.	*WAJIB* according to *Jumhur*.	*SUNNAH* according to *Shafites*.
7. *JAMA* of *Salat Ul Maghreb* and *Salat Ul Isha* at *Muzdalafah Jamat Takheer*.	*WAJIB* according to *Hanafites* so if he arrives there in *Maghreb* time, he or she must	*SUNNAH* according to *Jumhur*.

	still wait until *Isha*.		
8. *WUQUF* at *Muzdalafah*.	*WAJIB* after *Fajr* of the 10th of *Zul Hijjah* though if that is for a minute according to *Hanafites*.	*WAJIB* according to *Malikites* for such a time one can put away his or her belongings, eat, and pray *Maghreb* and *Isha* while stay for night is recommended. But it	*WAJIB* even if he stayed for a minute after midnight according to *Shafites* while according to *Hanbalites* stays for the last half of the night is *Wajib*.

		must be after midnight.	
9. *WUQUF* according to *Al Mashar Ul Haram* from *Fajr* to sunrise.	Recommended (*Mustahab*) according to *Hanafites*	*SUNNAH* according to *Jumhur*	
10. *Rami* of *Jamarat Ul Aqabah* on	< *WAJIB* unanimously >		

10th of *Zul Hijjah*.		
11. Shave or trim for men and cut for women.	*WAJIB* according to *Jumhur*.	*RUKN* according to Shafites
12. Sequence and order (*Tarteeb*) in *Rami*, *Zab'h* and *Halq*.	*WAJIB* according to *Hanafites*, but *Zab'h* in *Ifrad* is *Sunnah* so being of it in sequence is also *Sunnah*	*SUNNAH* according to *Jumhur*.

NOTE: *Zab'h* in *Ifrad* is *SUNNAH*. So far one in *Ifrad* the *Wajib*, *Tarteeb* is only in *Rami* and shave/trim.

13. *TAWAF IFADAH*.	*FARD* according to all, but the *Fard* part of it according to *Hanafites* are 4 rounds while the remaining three are *Wajib*, while according to Jumhur all 7 rounds are *Fard*.		
14. To do this *Tawaf* in *Ayyamun Nah'r*.	*WAJIB* according to *Hanafites*	*WAJIB* in the whole *Zul Hijjah* according to *Malikites*.	*SUNNAH* according to *Shafites* and *SUNNAH* on *Eid* day according to *Hanbalites*.
15. To do *Tawaf Ul Ifadah* after Rami on 10th.	*SUNNAH* according to *Jumhur*	*WAJIB* according to *Malikites*.	

NOTE: One can do it after *Rami* before *Zab'h*, but he or she cannot shave/trim his or her head or take off his *Ihram* before *Zab'h*. So, he or she has to do it in *Ihram*.

16. *RAMI* of all three	< *WAJIB* unanimously >

Jamarat in *Ayyamut Tashreeq*.			
17. Not to delay *RAMI* till night.	*SUNNAH* according to *Hanafites* and *Shafites*	*WAJIB* according to *Malikites*	*WAJIB* according to *Hanbalites* except in cases of stern need
18. Stay at *MINA* for the nights of *Tashreeq*.	*SUNNAH* according to *Hanafites*.	*WAJIB* according to *Jumhur*. The *Malikites* and *Shafites* exempted those in need like the bearer of water, etc.	
19. *TAWAF UL WIDA* for outsiders.	*WAJIB* according to *Jumhur*.	Recommended according to *Malikites*	

FARD IN *HAJJ*

1. *IHRAM*

Ihram means to enter into *Hurmah*, and *Hurmah* means *"sacredness and prohibition."* By doing so, certain things are prohibited now. While in a normal situation these are not, or the person concerned entered into sacredness and all these sanctioned in *Hajj* and *Umrah* are sacred. In the *Holy Quran*, *Allah* called it *Hurumat Ullah* and *Sha'aair Ullah*:

> *"Whoever will magnify (respect) the Hurumat [sacred] of Allah, so that is best for him (22:30 Holy Quran)."*

> *"Whoever will magnify [respect] the Sha'aair [signs] of Allah, so that is the piety of hearts (22:32 Holy Quran)."*

Also, whosoever put on *Ihram* cannot take it off until after doing *Umrah* or *Hajj*. But if he or she broke it he or she is bound to make *Qada*. For example, if one misses *Wuquf* at *Arafah*, he or she may do *Umrah* and take off his or her *Ihram*.

But if he was stopped from doing his *Hajj* or *Umrah*, he or she may slaughter a lamb and, later on, he or she will make *Qada*.

If someone who made intention for *Hajj* or *Umrah* became a *Muhrim* according to *Shafites* and *Hanbalites* and according to *Hanafites*, it is a must with the intention to say *Talbiyah* as well. However, *Malikites* said, if he or she put on *Ihram* and did not say *Talbiyah* he has become *Muhrim*, but he may slaughter a lamb or goat.

Then *Niyyah* is by heart, but it is recommended to say it out loud also as *Anas* narrated,

"I heard the Prophet saying:

Labbaik with Hajj and Umrah (Muslim).

The *Talbiyah* is –

Labbaika Allahumma Lbbaika La Shareeka Laka Labbaika Innal Hamda Wannimata Laka Wal Mulk La Shareeka Lak.

In *Niyat* one may specifically mention what he wants to do, the *Umrah*, the *Hajj* or both, as

Imam Bukhari and *Imam Muslim* both narrated a *Hadith* from *Aisha*:

> *Whoever wants to do Ihlal (make Ihram) for Hajj and Umrah may do that; whosoever wants to do Ihlal for Hajj may do that, and whoever wants to do Ihlal for Umrah may do that.*

However, if someone made intention for *Hajj* and did not mention whether this is *Naf'l* or *Fard*, then that is considered *Fard Hajj* by way of *Istihsan*. However, if he made intention for a *Naf'l Hajj*, then that is *Naf'l*. *Imam Shafi* said, if he or she mentions the *Naf'l*, that is still his *Fard*.

If someone puts on his or her *Ihram* and says, this is for *Manasik*, then according to *Abu Hanifa* he or she can make it for a specific *Ibadah* as long as he or she has not done *Tawaf*. But if he or she started *Tawaf* and completes one round, then that is *Umrah*.

The *Malikites* said if he has not mentioned anything and it was during the months of *Hajj*, it would be considered *Hajji Ifrad*. According to *Shafites* and *Hanbalites*, if he or she put on *Ihram* in the months of *Hajj* and did not mention anything but *Manasik*, then that *Tawaf* is considered *Qudum* if he wants it for *Hajj*. But if it was not in the months of *Hajj*, then that *Tawaf* is for *Umrah*. But according to one *Hanbalites* it may be in the months of *Hajj* or other months, it turned to *Tawaf Ul Umrah*, as if it was in the months of *Hajj*, then his *Hajj* will be the *Tamattu* as that is the best one according to them. Moreover, if the case was at a time other than the months of *Hajj*, then to turn it to *Hajj* is *Makrooh* or even prohibited at that time.

If someone forgot why he or she put on *Ihram*, it is allowed to turn it to whatever he or she wishes according to *Hanbalites*, but it should be before *Tawaf*, while *Jumhur* said it would be considered *Qiran*. This is based on another issue: whether it is allowed to turn *Hajj* to *Umrah* or not. According to *Hanbalites*, it is permitted, but not according to *Jumhur*.

Is it allowed to put a condition of *Tahallul*?

When someone says with intention the *Tahallul* time/place is where you ceased me. So, this is allowed according to *Shafites* and *Hanbalites* as except *Imam Bukhari*, five other *Muhaditheen* narrated from *Ibni Abbas* that *Duba'a Ibn Zubair* said,

> *"O the Messenger of Allah! "I am heavy and intend Hajj, so what do you advise me?"*

The Prophet said:

> *"Do Ihram and put condition."*

If someone made intention for two *Hajj* or two *Umrahs*, then that is for one only according to *Hanbalites* while according to *Jumhur* one would be done and, will make *Qada* for the other one later on. When one intends to put on *Ihram* he or she should bathe or at least make *Wudu*. *Imam Shafi* said if the water does not suffice for a bath or shower, but only for *Wudu*, then *Tayammum* after *Wudu* is an acceptable substitute.

Then this *ghusl* is for a woman in the period also, as *Abu Dawud* and *Tirmizi* narrated a *Hadith* from *Ibni Abbas* in this, she will do all *Manasik* except *Tawaf*.

Also for *Ihram* one has to cut one's nails and put on some fragrances according to *Hanafites* and *Hanbalites*. And on his or her *Ihram* cloth as well according to *Shafites* but that is not allowed neither on body nor *Ihram* cloth according to *Malikites*.

Imam Bukhari and *Imam Muslim* narrated from *Aisha*,

"As I was looking at the shine of the fragrance on the head of the Prophet."

While *Imam Malik* referred to another *Hadith* also narrated by *Imam Bukhari* and *Imam Muslim* from *Yala Ibni Umayyah*, someone came to the *Prophet* and asked him about who put on *Ihram* for *Umrah*, but his body had fragrance on it. The *Prophet* kept quiet for some time and then he said to wash the fragrance on his body.

But we say this case was in *Umrah* of *Ji'irranah* the eighth year after *Hijra* and the *Hadith* of *Aisha* is in *Hajjat Ul Wida*, 10th year. Also, according to *Shafites* and *Hanbalites* the women should put *Khidab* (henna) on their hands before *Ihram* as *Ibni Umar* said this is *Sunnah*. Before intention and after putting on *Ihram* dress, he or she may pray two *Rakat* prayers, according to all schools. Also, the *Malikites* and *Hanbalites* said, donning *Ihram* could happen after a *Fard* prayer. *Imam Bukhari* and *Imam Muslim* narrated that the *Prophet* prayed two *Rakat* at *Zul Hulaifa* and then made his intention. Also, it is *Sunnah* to pray *Surat Ul Kafirun* in the first *Rakat* and *Surat Ul Ikhlas* in the second *Rakat*.

> *Ibni Abbas narrated that the Prophet did Ihram when he finished his prayer (Fard prayer) (Abu Dawud).*

Also, it is allowed to make intention according to *Hanbalites* when one starts his or her travel. This is best according to *Malikites* and *Shafites* to make *Ihram* i.e. intention when the ride starts, *as Imam Muslim* narrated from *Jabir*

> *"The Prophet commanded us to make intention when we face the direction [start traveling]."*

He may say *Talbiyah* after the prayer as the *Prophet* did (*Tirmizi, Nisa'i*). This is according to *Hanafites*. It is also permissible to say it when one starts traveling. According to *Shafites*, one may say *Talbiyah* with intention and according to *Malikites* and *Hanbalites Talbiyah* should be made when he takes his or her ride. Then to say as much *Talbiyah* as he can is recommended as *Ibni Umar* said from the *Prophet* that –

> *The best* Hajj *is the louder voice (with Talbiyah) and slaughter (Tirmizi, Ibni Majah).*

Then one may stop *Talbiyah* with *Tawaf*, but restart it after *Sai* until *Zawal* time on *Arafah*, as this practice is narrated from *Ali* and *Ummi Salmah*. This is according to *Malikites*.

Jumhur said he might stop it with the start of *Rami* on the 10th of *Zul Hijjah*, as the *Prophet* was saying *Talbiyah* until he started *Rami* (*Bukhari, Muslim* from *Fadl Ibni Abbas*).

This is because *Tahallul* (to become *Halal*) takes place with *rami* according to *Hanafites*. It is the case if he or she has done *Rami* before shave / trim, but if he shaved / trimmed before *Rami* then he or she may stop it with the shave /

trim as he has become *Halal* with that. In *Umrah* one may stop *Talbiyah* with the start of *Tawaf*.

1. *WUQUF* AT *ARAFAH*

Wuquf means stay and not to stand there.

The *Prophet* said:

Hajj is "Arafah (Tirmizi, Abu Dawud, Nisa'i, Ibni Majah)."

This is the main *Ruk'n* of *Hajj*, so anyone who misses this *Wuquf* has missed the *Hajj*. The whole *Arafah* is the place for *Wuquf*. The time for *Wuquf* is from the *Zawal* on the 9th of *Zul Hijjah* until daybreak on the 10th of *Zul Hijjah*. According to *Hanbalites*, the time starts with daybreak on the 9th until daybreak on the 10th. The *Prophet* said after that he prayed *Fajr* prayer on 10th:

"Whosoever attended this prayer with us and stayed with us till we go, and he already did Wuquf *at Arafah before this either day time or night time, then his* Hajj *is completed (Muslim, Abu Dawud, Tirmizi, Nisa'i, Ibni Majah)."*

If someone did *Wuquf* at *Arafah* on the 9th before *Zawal*, then left before *Zawal* and did not come back to *Arafah* until the break of dawn, he or she has missed the *Hajj*. If someone was sleeping or unconscious on his or her ride and passed by *Arafah* anytime after *Zawal*, and did not know that it was *Arafah*, his or her *Wuquf* is still done, according to *Hanafites,* while *Shafites* and *Hanbalites* have the same view regarding someone who was sleeping or who did not know this is *Arafah*. But someone who was unconscious drunk lost his senses, then there is no *Ibadah* for a senseless person. This time is to be considered from *Fajr* at 9th until *Fajr* at 10th according to *Hanbalites*.

It is *Wajib* according to *Hanafites* and *Hanbalites* to stay there until sunset on the 9th to have his or her stay at day and night combined, as the *Prophet* did this. So, if one left *Arafat* before sunset, then he or she is bound to give *Dum*, while that is *Sunnah* according to *Shafites*.

According to *Malikites* for one who is passing by *Arafah* it is a must to know this is *Arafat* and to have the intention of presence there. However, this is not the case if one is unconscious as his or her *Wuquf* is done without intention and knowledge. To them, the *Ruk'n* of *Hajj* is *Wuquf* at *Arafat* on the night of the 10th of *Zul Hijjah*. So, if someone came out before sunset on the 9th and did not go back to *Arafat* before daybreak on the night of the 10th, he or she has missed the *Hajj*. However, another saying like that of *Hanafites* and *Hanbalites* is that if he or she came out before sunset and never came back, he or she may give a *Dum*. According to *Shafites* and *Hanbalites*, that *Dum* is *Sunnah*. Then it is enough to do *Wuquf* for a little while. However, according to *Malikites*, it may be at least like the time of sitting in between two *Sajdahs*.

THE *SUNNAH* OF *WUQUF*

I. It is *Sunnah* to start going to *Arafat* on the 9th of *Zul Hijjah* after sunrise at *Mina*.

II. To pray *Zuhr* and *Asr* at *Zuhr* time with one *Azan* and two *Iqamahs* without any separation of the two by praying *Sunnah* or *Naf'l* in between. This *Jama* of two prayers is for everyone in *Hajj* according to *Hanbalites*.

Even if he is from *Makkah*, and for each one even the inhabitants of *Arafah* according to *Malikites*. *Qasr* of both prayers is for everyone except the people of *Makkah* and *Arafah*, as they are not travelers according to *Hanbalites*. Moreover, *Qasr* is not allowed for people of *Arafat* according to *Malikites*. They will pray both prayers at *Zuhr* time fully and with two *Azans* without *Naf'l* in between, but they have allowed *Qasr* for *Makki*. According to *Shafites* this *Jama* and *Qasr* both are not because of *Hajj*, but because of traveling, so if one in *Hajj* stayed at *Makkah* for four days with the intention to stay as this is the minimum days to be considered *Muqeem*, then came to *Arafat* with the intention of coming back to *Makkah*, they may pray both prayers completely and in its own time, but if their intention is to go back to their countries from that place, then they may do both *Qasr* and *Jama* as a traveler.

To *Hanafites*, *qasr* is because of travel and *Jama* is because of being behind the *Imam* of *Hajj*. So, if someone is not a traveler he or she may pray both prayers completely, and one who is not behind the *Imam* of *Hajj* is not allowed to do *Jama* of both prayers. He must pray both in their times.

III. To bathe at *Namirah* if possible.

IV. Not to enter *Arafat* before *Zawal* but to stay at *Namirah*, which is not part of *Arafat* like the *Ornah* valley.

V. For *Imam* to give two *Khutbahs* and to do *Jama* between the two prayers, so he or she must be a traveler, not a local.

VI. To go to *Arafat* for *Wuquf* right after *Zawal* and prayer.

VII. It is best to stay at the bottom of *Jabal Ur Rahmah* (the mountain) near the big rocks.

VIII. To remain in *Arafat* until sunset is *Sunnah* according to *Shafites*, but *Wajib* according to *Jumhur*.

IX. To face *Qiblah* with *Taharah*, *Sat'r*, and with intention. This intention is not *Shart* because *Wuquf* takes place in the same *ihram* of *Hajj*. So, his intention for *Hajj* is enough. But *Tawaf Ul Ifadah* takes place after *Tahallul*, so it needs intention; if someone did *Wuquf* without *Taharah*, even in *Junabat*, or a woman did it menstrual cycle or someone did it without *Sat'r*, their *Wuquf* is done.

X. Fasting is not recommended for one in *Hajj*.

XI. It is *Sunnah* to do as much *Ibadat* and *Duas* as one can.

2. *TAWAF*

As we know that *Umrah* has its own *Tawaf*. That is the only *Ruk'n* of *Umrah* according to *Hanafites* and one of the *Arkan* according to *Jumhur* while *Hajj* has:

i. *Tawaf Ul Qudum* – This is the first ever practice one has to do when he or she arrives in *Makkah*, and he or she had the *Ihram* for *Hajji Ifrad*. This *Tawaf* is *Sunnah* according to *Jumhur* and *Wajib* according to *Malikites*, if one has time to do it, and he or she is not going to miss *Wuquf* at *Arafat*. So, if someone went straight to *Arafat* without *Tawaf-I-Qudum*, he may slaughter a lamb, as this is *Jenayat* according to *Malikites*. But if the time is short, then this is not *Wajib*. *Tawaf-I-Qudum* is all right if he or she intended a *Naf'l Tawaf*. However, according to *Malikites* he or she may make another *Tawaf* with the intention of *Qudum* or of *Wajib*, and he may repeat his *Sai* also, if he has done it after that *Naf'l Tawaf* for *Hajj*.

This *Tawaf* is *Sunnah* for one who intended for *Hajji Qiran* according to *Hanafites* and he will do this after his *Umrah's Tawaf* and *Sai*. However, according to *Jumhur*, *Tawaf* of *Umrah* can suffice for this *Tawaf* if he or she did not do another one.

a) There is no *Tawaf-I-Qudum* or *Tawaf Ul Ifadah* in *Umrah*.

b) For a *Makki* or one from *Hil* area there is no *Tawaf-I-Qudum*; For him or her, but according to *Malikites* one who put on his *ihram* from *Hil* even though if he is a *Makki* may do *Tawaf Ul Qudum*, as this is *Wajib*.

- c) Near *Hanbalites* one in *Tamattu* may do *Tawaf Ul Qudum* before *Tawaf Ul Ifadah*.

- d) According to *Shafites*, one who entered *Makkah* from outside even though he or she is without *ihram* may do this *Tawaf* as this is like *Tahiyyatul Masjid* for *Baitullah*.

ii. *Tawaf Ul Ifadah* is also called *Tawaf Ul Hajj*, *Tawaf Uz Ziyarah* or *Tawafur Ruk'n* as this is the *Ruk'n* of *Hajj* as *Allah* said:

And they may make Tawaf of the Ancient House (22:29).

This *Tawaf* is *Fard*, so if someone misses it, he or she must come back to do that whenever possible and for its delay he or she must slaughter.

The time for this *Tawaf* starts at daybreak on the 10th of *Zul Hijjah*. However, the *Sunnah* way of this *Tawaf* is when the one in *Hajj* does *rami* of *Jamarat Ul Aqabah*, and does *Qurbani* in the case of *Tamattu*, and *Qiran*. Now if he or she wants, he or she can do this *Tawaf* in *ihram* before the shave / trim. This is better, according to some scholars, or to shave / trim his or her hair and then to do it in regular dress.

iii. *Tawaf Ul Wida*, which is also called *Tawaf Us Sadr*. This is *Wajib* according to *Jumhur* and recommended according to *Malikites*. *Imam Tirmizi* narrates from *Ibni Umar*:

Whoever performed *Hajj* of *Baitullah*, his last deed may be this house (*Tawaf* of this house), except women in period as the prophet gave them permission (to go back without it).

So, if one has traveled less than the distance of *Qasr*, he or she should come back and do it, so his or her *Wajib* is done. If he or she has gone far, then he or she should send a sacrifice, as missing of a *Wajib* in *Hajj* will cause it, according to *Shafites* and *Hanbalites*, while according to *Hanafites* if he or she has gone out of *Meeqat* then he or she may send a sacrifice. But even in the case of coming back, the *Shafites* said, a sacrifice is due.

Saeed Ibni Mansur narrated in his *Sunan* (Book of *Hadith*) that *Umar* sent one person back to *Makkah* from *Marruz Zahran* to perform it. This *Tawaf* is only on those who are from areas outside *Mawaqeet* according to *Hanafites*, while according to *Hanbalites* this is *Wajib* on those living outside the limits of *Haram*. And to *Shafites*, this is *Wajib* on everyone going out of *Makkah* even though if they are from *Makkah*. If they are going on an extended trip, or a short one, as the *Hadith* of *Ibni Abbas* says:

No one may go out, but his last deed may be this House (Ahmad, Abu Dawud, Muslim, Ibni Majah).

And the same is recommended for a *Makki* according to *Malikites* as well. The time of this *Tawaf* is after *Tawaf Ul Ifadah*; then according to *Hanafites* it could even be done with the *Niyat* of a *Naf'l Tawaf*, but according to *Shafites* and *Hanbalites* it needs a specific intention. To *Malikites* if someone made the intention of this with *Tawaf Ul Ifadah* then that is done. Near *Jumhur* it may be done as the last deed after *Hajj* so if one did it, and then stayed at *Makkah* more, he or she may repeat it.

If someone missed *Tawaf Ul Ifadah*, he or she has missed the *Hajj*, but *Malikites* said that *Tawaf Ul Qudum* could cover this missing component. Yes, if he has missed *Tawaf Ul Ifadah*, but he has done *Tawaf Ul Wida*, then that one can cover it because this *Tawaf* is done after the time of *Tawaf Ul Ifadah*. But according to *Jumhur*, *Tawaf Ul Qudum* was before the time of *Ifadah*, so it cannot cover *Tawaf Ul Ifadah*.

HOW TO DO *TAWAF*?

Tawaf starts from the corner of *Hajar-I-Aswad*. He or she will kiss it or touch it with hand and kiss the hand or by *Istilam* to face it raising his or her hands and say, "*Allahu Akbar.*" Then he will start walking around the *Ka'ba*, keeping the *Ka'ba* on the left side, making *Dua* or reciting from the *Qur'an*. When he or she comes to *Rukni Yamani*, he or she does its *Istilam* as well. But in *Istilam* of *Hajari Aswad* he or she has to kiss his or her hands, but not in the case of *Rukni-Yamani*. He or she will finish his or her round with *Hajari Aswad* and will start the second round as he or she did for the first one. After the 7th round at the end of *Tawaf* once again he or she will do *Istilam* of *Hajari Aswad*. This one is considered like *Salam* in prayer.

SHURUT OF TAWAF

1. *Taharat* is *Shart* according to *Jumhur* as *Tawaf* is like prayer, so it needs *Taharat*.

The *Prophet* said:

Tawaf of the House (of Allah) is prayer. But Allah has allowed talking therein, so whosoever wants to talk, he may not but good only (Hakim, Ibni Hibban).

But according to *Hanafites*, *Taharat* for *Tawaf* is *Wajib*. Because when talking is allowed therein, then it means it is not all like prayer, and *Imam Tirmizi* narrated the *Hadith*:

Tawaf around the house is like prayer.

So, it is not all alike, so if someone did it without *Taharat* then as long as one is at *Makkah* he or she must repeat it with *Taharat*. If he or she did the same in *Ayyamun Nah'r* 10th, 11th and 12th, then his or her *Tawaf* is acceptable, but if he or she delayed and then did it later on, then he or she may slaughter a lamb or goat, and if he or she did not repeat it so if he or she has done it without *Wudu* then he or she may slaughter a lamb. But if he or she has done it in *Junabat* then he may slaughter a *Budana* (cow or camel). Someone according to *Shafites* who cannot use water can do it with *Tayammum*. But if he or she was still in *Makkah* or has returned to *Makkah*, then if he or she can use water, he or she may do so. If the *Wudu* of someone is broken in the middle of *Tawaf* he may make his *Wudu* and complete his *Tawaf*.

2. *Satar* - To cover the *Aurah*. It is also a *Shart* according to *Jumhur*, *Malikites*, *Shafites* and *Hanbalites* as *Tawaf* is all alike prayer according to them and also the *Prophet* said:

   A naked one may not make Tawaf of the house (Bukhari, Muslim).

However, to *Hanafites* this *Hadith* was regarding the practice of *Mushrikeen*, as they used to do *Tawaf* naked, so the case of *Satar* is just like the case of *Taharat*.

3. The intention for *Tawaf* is *Shart* according to *Hanafites*, but not the specification, while that is *Shart* and specifically according to *Shafites*. For a *Tawaf* which is not part of

Hajj and that is *Tawaf Ul Wida*, then the specific intention is *Shart* according to *Hanbalites* for each *Tawaf*. That is not a *Shart* according to *Malikites*, but the intention of *Hajj* suffices it.

4. To do *Tawaf* on foot if one does not have a legitimate excuse is also *Shart* according to *Hanafites* and *Hanbalites*, while it is *Wajib* according to *Malikites* and *Sunnah* according to *Shafites*. According to *Hanafites* and *Hanbalites*, if he or she has done it on a ride without excuse, he or she may remake it as long as he or she is at *Makkah*, but if he or she went back without remaking it then he or she may pay *Dum* (sacrifice), and according to *Malikites* there is no remaking, but *Dum* only.

5. *Tawaf* may be inside the *Masjid Ul Haram* according to all schools and one may do it outside the *Hateem* as that is the part of the house.

6. To start *Tawaf* from *Hajari Aswad* is *Shart* according to *Shafites* and *Hanbalites* and *Wajib* according to *Hanafites* and *Malikites*.

7. To have the *Ka'ba* to one's left when he or she is making *Tawaf* is *Shart* according to *Jumhur* and *Wajib* according to *Hanafites*.

8. The time of *Tawaf Ul Ifadah* starts at daybreak of *Yaumun Nah'r*, the 10th of *Zul Hijjah* according to *Hanafites* and *Malikites*, while its time starts after midnight, the night of the 10th, according to *Shafites* and *Hanbalites*. But if he delayed it from the 12th, then a *Dum* is due according to *Hanafites*.

9. All seven rounds are *Fard* according to *Jumhur*, but according to *Hanafites*, the significant portion of rounds is *Fard*, i.e., four rounds while remaining three is *Wajib*.

10. To make the rounds consistently is *Shart* according to *Malikites* and *Hanbalites*. But according to *Hanafites* and *Shafites*, that is *Sunnah*. If something happened to him or her in *Tawaf* he or she shall remake his *Wudu* and complete the *Tawaf*, but according to *Malikites* and *Hanbalites,* if there was a long interval then he may restart it from the beginning. To them, even *Salat Ul Janazah* and a *Naf'l* prayer breaks *Tawaf*.

11. To pray two *Rakat*s after completion of *Tawaf* is *Wajib* according to *Hanafites* and *Malikites*. But according to *Hanafites*, it is not allowed in prohibited times to pray like after *Fajr* prayer and *Asr* prayer. These two *Rakats* are *Sunnah* according to *Shafites* and *Hanbalites*.

IMPORTANT ISSUES REGARDING WOMEN IN *HAJJ*

When the menstrual period of a woman starts before *Ihram,* then from *Meeqat* she will put on *Ihram* after bathing. Then she will do everything except *Tawaf*, as that is inside the *Masjid*. But if her period started after *Ihram*, then there is no need for a shower. The *Prophet* ordered *Aisha* to do whatever the others are doing except *Tawaf*, as narrated by *Imam Bukhari* and *Imam Muslim*.

As far as *Tawaf-I-Qudum* is concerned for a menstruating woman, there is nothing on her if she misses it, but only according to *Malikites* as this *Tawaf* is *Wajib* according to them. In the case of *Tamattu*, she will put on *Ihram* for *Hajj* and her *Hajj* will become *Qiran* according to *Jumhur*. While *Imam Abu Hanifa* said, her *Umrah* is dropped, and she will do *ihram* for *Hajj*, as the *Prophet* ordered *Aisha*. He told her to comb her hair and put on *Ihram* for *Hajj* and leave *Umrah*.

And when she made *Umrah* from *Tan'eem* as she was asking to, then the *Prophet* said to her that this *Umrah* is a substitute to your *Umrah*. But the *Prophet* himself did not order her to make *Umrah*. Moreover, if a woman is in a hurry to leave *Makkah*, but she is on her menstrual period and unable to make *Tawaf Ul Ifadah*, she may take a shower and then make *Tawaf* and *Sai*, and she will slaughter a *Budana* (a cow of two years or more or a camel of 5 years or more) according to *Hanafites*. Now this practice has been adopted by the followers of the other three imams also.

SUNNAH OF TAWAF

(i) **_ISTILAM_** of *Hajari Aswad*:

One must touch it with both hands or just the right hand at the beginning of each round, if this is possible without harming anybody, and to kiss the hand. Or if one can kiss the *Hajar* directly, he or she should do that. If he cannot do these, then he may indicate to it, i.e., raise one or both hands towards it and kiss it. According to *Shafites*, this kiss should be three times and he should say *Takbeer* and *Tahleel*. The kiss is cited by *Imam Bukhari* and *Muslim* from the Prophet, and *Shafites* said if one can do, he may put his forehead over it, as *Imam Bayhaqi* related this as the practice of the *Prophet*.

The *Prophet Muhammad* said to *Umar*,

You are a strong man, do not push or pull over Hajar. You will harm a weak one (Shafi and Ahmad).

Nafi said,

"I saw Ibni Umar doing Istilam of Hajari Aswad, and said since I have seen the Prophet did it, I have never missed it"

While *Abu Dawud* and *Nisa'i* related from *Ibni Umar* that the *Prophet* used not to leave *Istilam* of *Rukni Yamani* and *Hajari Aswad*. But the kissing of *Rukni Yamani* is not a practice; only *Istilam* of that either by touch or by indication.

(ii) **_DUA_** –

Dua means whatever you want to ask, as *Allah* is happy with one who invokes Him. So, if someone will adopt these *Duas* the *Prophet* made it, that is good but in between *Rukni Yamani* and *Hajari Aswad*, it is *Sunnah* to say:

Rabbana Atina Fid Dunya Hasanah Wa Fil Aakirati Hasanah Waqina Azaban Nar.

And if someone does not have these *Duas*, then he or she should recite whatever he or she has from *Quran*.

(iii) **_RAM'L_** –

This *Ram'l* is for men in the first three rounds to move their shoulders, according to *Hanafites* and *Shafites*; this is *Sunnah* in each *Tawaf* having *Sai* after and he is in *Ihram*. So, if someone has done his *Sai* after *Tawaf I Qudum* then he is in no need of *Ram'l* in *Tawaf Ul Ifadah*, even though if he is doing that in *ihram* and if he has not done *Sai* before and he will do it after *Tawaf Ul Ifadah*, but he is in his dress then again there is no need for *Ram'l*. According to *Malikites* and *Hanbalites* *Ram'l* is *Sunnah* in *Qudum* and in *Umrah* as the *Prophet* did it in *Qudum* and made *Sai* after that.

Imams Bukhari and *Muslim* related that the *Prophet* did it in the first three rounds. It should not be left without excuse, but if he or she misses it, then there is no *Qada*. *Ram'l* is for one who did his *Ihram* for *Umrah* and *Hajj* from *Meeqat*, this is *Sunnah* and for others, it is recommended.

(iv) ***ID'TIBA***

Id'tiba is to pass the right side of the upper cloak of *Ihram* under one's right shoulder, as *Abu Dawud, Ibni Maja* and *Tirmizi* narrated this practice from the *Prophet*, and *Ahmad* and *Abu Dawud* narrated from *Ibni Abbas* that the *Prophet* and his companions did *Id'tiba* when they did *Ihram* from *Ji'irranah*. This is *Sunnah* according to *Jumhur* in a *Tawaf* he is doing *Ram'l* therein. *Id'tiba* will be in all seven rounds. According to *Shafites*, this is *Sunnah* in *Sai'* also even though if he has missed it in *Tawaf*. But there is no *Ram'l* on a *Makki*. According to *Malikites*, *Id'tiba* is not *Sunnah*.

(v) To make *Tawaf* close to *Baitullah* is also *Sunnah* according to *Hanafites* and *Malikites*. But this is recommended according to *Shafites* and *Hanbalites*.

(vi) To make *Tawaf* on foot is *Sunnah* according to *Shafites* and *Hanbalites* and *Wajib* according to *Hanafites* and *Malikites*.

(vii) To pray two *Rakat* after *Tawaf* is *Sunnah* according to *Shafites* and *Hanbalites* and *Wajib* according to *Hanafites* and *Malikites*. To *Hanbalites* if someone prayed the *Fard* prayer after *Tawaf*, then there is no need of these two *Rakat*.

(viii) The intention for *Tawaf Ul Qudum* and *Tawaf Ul Ifadah* is *Sunnah* because these are part of *Hajj*, but it is *Wajib* for *Wida* according to *Shafites*. The *Hanafites* said for *Ifadah* intention is *Shart*, as this is performed after *Tahallul*.

SAI

Sai in between *Safa* and *Marwah* is *Ruk'n* according to *Jumhur* and *Wajib* according to *Hanafites* as the *Prophet* said:

> *Moreover, He (Allah) prescribed for you the "Sai" so do Sai.*

a) *WAJIBAT OF SAI*

Its Wajibat are as follows

i. For one who has done a correct *Tawaf* before it, but according to *Hanafites* if someone did it after that he has done four rounds of *Tawaf* then that is also done. According to *Jumhur*, one can do it after any *Tawaf*, but according to *Shafites*, it can be done after *Qudum* or *Ifadah* only.

ii. To start it with *Safa* and to finish it with *Marwah*.

The *Prophet* said:

> *Start with what Allah has started with (Nisa'i).*

iii. To make seven rounds is *Fard* according to *Jumhur* while four Rounds are *Wajib* according to *Hanafites* and the remaining is *Sunnah*.

iv. To do it in consistency is *Shart* according to *Malikites* and *Hanbalites* and *Sunnah* according to *Hanafites* and *Shafites*.

v. Specification of intention and walking on foot are also *Shurut* according to *Hanbalites*, but *Taharat* is not a *Shart* for *Sai* and that is why a woman in period or even one in *Junabat* if did it, that is done.

b) *SUNNAH* OF *SA'I*

i. To do *Istilam* of *Hajari Aswad* after *Tawaf* and to pray two *Rakat* after *Tawaf*, and then next to go for *Sai* from *Safa Gate* (*Babus Safa*) to follow the *Sunnah*.

ii. To do it after *Tawaf* without any big interval and also to make the rounds of *Sai* consistently, so if he or she did *Tawaf* today and then *Sai* tomorrow, that is all right. There is no *Sunnah* prayer after *Sai*.

iii. *Tahara*t and *Sat'r* are *Sunnah* for *Sai*.

iv.	Walking if he does not have any excuse.
v.	To go up to *Safa* and *Marwah*.
vi.	*Dua* is *Sunnah* and if he made it from *Ahadith* that is recommended.
vii.	To walk swiftly (light running or jogging) in between the green lights from both side. Then *Sai* should be in *Ayyamun-Nah'r* after *Tawaf*, but if he or she delayed it still that is its time, so that is all right. If he goes back to his or her country, then he or she has missed it and must give a *Dum*. But if he comes back in a new *Ihram* and makes it, then his *Dum* is dropped even if he or she engaged in sexual intercourse, and then he did *Sai* that is ok. All this is according to *Hanafites* because *Sai* is *Wajib* according to *Hanafites*.

WAJIBAT OF *HAJJ*

There are two *Wajibat* according to *Hanafites* for *Umrah*:

(1) *Sai* and

(2) Shave / Trim while for *Hajj* these are as follows:

i. *Sai*

ii. *Wuquf* at *Muzdalafah* at daybreak in between the 9th and 10th days.

iii. The *rami*.

iv. *Zab'h/Qurbani* for one performing *Tamattu* or *Qiran*.

v. Shave/Trim

vi. *Tarteeb* (order) in *Rami* of *Jamarat Ul Aqabah* on the 10th day, then *Zab'h* and then shave/trim. To perform *Tawaf Ul Ifadah* after these three is *Sunnah*.

vii. *Tawaf Ul Wida* for outsiders

viii. *Wuquf* at *Arafah* to have sunsets there. According to *Malikites* the *Wajib* in *Umrah* is shave / trim only, while in *Hajj* these are:

a) *Tawaf Ul Qudum.*

b) *Wuquf* at *Muzdalafah.*

c) *Rami*

d) Shave/Trim

e) Spend the nights in *Mina.*

According to *Shafites* in *Umrah*, there is only one *Wajib* if he is a *Makki* all others are *Arkan* and *Fard*, while in *Hajj* the *Wajibat* are:

i. *Ihram* from *Meeqat.*

ii. *Rami*

iii. *Wuquf* at *Muzdalafah.*

iv. Stay at *Mina* at nights.

v. *Tawaf Ul Wida.* According to *Hanbalites* the *Wajib* in *Umrah* are two:

a) *Ihram* from *Hil* if he is a *Makki*, and

b) Shave/Trim.

While in *Hajj Wajibat* are:

(1) *Ihram* from *Meeqat*.

(2) *Wuquf* at *Arafah* to have sunsets there

(3) *Wuquf* at *Muzdalafah* after midnight

(4) Spend the nights at *Mina*

(5) *Rami* in sequence to throw pebbles on *Jamarat Us Sughra*, then *Wasta* then *Kubra/Aqabah*.

(6) Shave / Trim, and

(7) *Tawaf Ul Wida*.

WUQUF AT *MUZDALAFAH*

This would be like *Wuquf* at *Arafat*, so if someone happens there accidentally but in *Wuquf's* time, he or she is sleeping or unconscious or passes by and does not make any intention of *Wuquf*, even if he or she does not know that this is *Muzdalafah*, his or her *Wajib* is done according to *Hanafites,* while according to *Malikites* to get down of the ride and to put down his belongings and to eat or drink a little, or to be there on the ground to the extent of these actions is *Wajib*, so if he or she does not come down but only passes by, then he or she is bound to give *Dum*.

The *Shafites* said it is enough to be there even if he or she passes by it but after midnight as that is the *Wuquf* time. The *Hanbalites* said, to stay there at night is *Wajib*, but to leave before midnight is not allowed. After midnight, it is allowed in some circumstances, as

Ibni Abbas said,

> "I came to Mina before the Prophet with those in need."

Also, he allowed *Asma* to go before.

To be with *Taharah* is not a *Shart*. Then the whole *Muzdalafah* is a place for *Wuquf* except *Muhassar* Valley. It is *Makrooh* to do *Wuquf* there according to *Hanafites*. The time of *Wuquf* according to *Hanafites* is in between daybreak of the 10th day and sunrise, so as long it lasts one may stay there for a while at daybreak. To stay at night is *Sunnah*, but if he or she left for *Mina* after daybreak without praying *Fajr*, he or she did wrong and his or her *Wajib* is done.

To *Malikites Wuquf* to the extent of coming down from the ride, *Maghreb* and *Isha* prayers and to the extent of eating a little in any part of the night is enough for *Wajib*. However, *Sunnah* is to stay at night there.

The *Shafites* said, *Wajib* is to do this *Wuquf* for a little time after midnight and if he or she does not, then he or she may give *Dum*. Also, the *Hanbalites* said, spending the night in *Muzdalafah* is *Wajib* until dawn break. Then if someone leaves *Muzdalafah* with good reason before dawn breaks, his *Wuquf* is done, but if someone leaves without reason, then he or she is to slaughter a lamb, while *Jumhur* said, missing *Wuquf* at *Muzdalafah* causes *Dum* (sacrifice).

THE *SUNNAH* OF *WUQUF* AT *MUZDALAFAH*:

i. To take a shower there is recommended.

ii. To pray *Maghreb* and *Isha* there in time of *Isha* with two *Iqamahs* in *Jama'ah* or even individually.

iii. This is recommended if he or she can take pebbles from there, 70 in total if he or she wants to stay there for all *Ayyamun Nah'r*, but only 49 if he or she wants to leave *Mina* on the 12th to wash it, is recommended according to *Nawawi* as *Ibni Umar* did it.

iv. *Wuquf* according to *Mash 'Arul Haram* (mountain)

v. To pray *Fajr* right after dawn break.

vi. *Wuquf* according to *Mash 'Arul Haram* after *Fajr* prayer facing *Ka'ba*, say *Takbeer*, *Tahleel*, *Talbiyah* and make *Dua* then leave for *Mina* before sunrise.

vii. Near *Shafites*, it is *Sunnah* to send weak and sick people before *Fajr* to do *Rami*.

viii. To pass *Muhassar* valley swiftly as this is the place where the companions of elephants were hit by *Allah*.

STAY AT *MINA* AND *RAMI*

Rami is a symbolic action to express that one counters Satan, as one hates him. This is to follow the *Sunnah* of *Ibrahim*, *Ismail* and *Hajar,* as they did it in these places when Satan tried to whisper to them regarding the *Zab'h* of *Ismail*. This is the commandment of *Allah*. The limits of *Mina* are in between *Jamrat Ul Aqabah* and *Muhassar* valley. The *Rami* is *Wajib* to follow the practice of the *Prophet*. If someone has a reasonable excuse, he or she can ask another to do *Rami* on his or her behalf so that the agent will do his or her *Rami first* and then the *Rami* of his or her client. With the *Rami* of each pebble, he may say *Allahu Akbar*. In this case the client is to give *Dum* according to *Malikites*.

On 10th of *Zul Hijjah* the time of *Rami* of *Jamarat Ul Aqabah* starts after sunrise according to *Hanafites* and *Malikites*, as the *Prophet* said when he sent the weaker people of his family with *Ibni Abbas* at night from *Muzdalafah* to *Mina*:

> *Do not do* rami *till sunrise (Muslim, Abu Dawud, Tirmizi, Nisa'i, Ibni Majah).*

However, according to *Shafites* and *Hanbalites*, its time starts at midnight (on the night of the 10th), as *Abu Dawud* narrated that the *Prophet* ordered *Ummi Salmah* to do it at night, so she did it before daybreak, and then she went and performed *Tawaf*.

Then according to *Jumhur*, *Talbiyah* may be stopped with the first pebble he throws as *Fadl Ibni Abbas* said:

> *I was on a ride behind the Prophet from Muzdalafah to Mina, so he was saying Talbiyah till rami (Bukhari, Muslim, Abu Dawud, Tirmizi, Nisa'i, Ibni Majah)."*

While according to *Malikites*, *Talbiyah* is stopped on the 9th of *Zul Hijjah* at *Zawal* time. This continues till the end of the day as *Imam Bukhari* narrates that one man said to the *Prophet* that he did *rami* after *Zawal*, the *Prophet* said that is not a sin. R*ami* on the 11th and 12th starts after *Zawal*, as *Ibni Abbas* said that the *Prophet* did *rami* at *Zawal* time (*Ahmad, Tirmizi,* and *Abu Maja*). This continues until sunset, but if someone delays that he or she can do it at night before *Fajr*, while this delay will cause him or her *Dum* according to *Malikites*. The *Shafites* said one can do it the next day or on any day until the 13th; even if he has missed *Rami* on the 10th, he can do it on the 11th, 12th, or 13th. And *Hanbalites* said this is not allowed except for people in need; and according to *Shafites* this delay until night for those in need may not be for two days, but only for one day.

Then on the 12th, when someone wants to leave *Mina*, that is allowed, but it is better to stay for another night, as *Allah* said:

> *Then whoever hastened in two days, then there is no sin on him and whosoever delayed [for another day] then there is no sin on him for one who fears [Allah] (2:2-3).*

If someone was at *Mina* on the 12th at sunset, he or she cannot leave *Mina*, but must stay for the night and do *rami* the next day as well. This is according to *Jumhur* while according to

Hanafites he can go, from *Mina* until before dawn break. One who stayed there or remained there for 13th, then according to *Jumhur* the time of *rami* is the same time, i.e., *Zawal*. But according to *Hanafites* that is allowed before *Zawal* also, as *Ibni Abbas* said:

> *When the day is started the last day of Tashreeq then "Rami is permitted.*

a) *Rami* may be with anything from the nature of the earth like stone, clay, even a handful of dust, but it will be considered one pebble. This is according to *Hanafites*, but according to *Jumhur* it may only be with stones. The stones may be little bigger than garbanzo beans, but not too big, and when they fall near *Jamrah*, that is also acceptable.

b) Order in *Jamarat* is *Sunnah* according to *Hanafites*, so if someone misses the order, his or her *Wajib* is done. However, this is not the case according to *Jumhur*. Every *Jamrah* may be hit with seven pebbles every day, but according to *Hanbalites* if someone hits one or two fewer, that is acceptable. If someone is in doubt about the number of pebbles, he or she should consider the lesser number. Taking pebbles from *Mina* or any other place is allowed, but *Sunnah* is from *Muzdalafah*, as the *Prophet* ordered *Ibni Abbas* to take it from *Muzdalafah*. But to take it from another place than *Muzdalafah* is *Makrooh* according to *Hanbalites*. However, according to *Hanafites* if someone took the same stones that hit *Jamrah* once, that is *Makrooh* and not allowed according to *Jumhur*, as there is a *Hadith* that said:

Do Rami with and that is not a sin.

But as the *Prophet* said when *Abu Saeed* asked him about these stones:

Indeed, whatever is accepted of it been lifted and, it would not have been the case, you would have seen it like mountains (Dari Qutni, Hakim).

Rami should be on one's right hand and to hit *Jamarat Ul Aqabah* it is recommended to keep

Makkah to the left and *Mina* to the right. Then any *Jamrah* followed by another one, one has to make *Dua* there, but not after *Aqabah* if the sequence is followed.

Rami is *Wajib*, so if someone misses it, he may give *Dum*. If he or she left the major portion of a *Rami*, it means he hit three stones and left four, and he or she may give *Dum* as well according to *Hanafites*. If he missed the lesser part, then for each stone he left, he may pay a *Sadaqah* of half of a *Sa* (a pot used for grain), and half of a *Sa* is 1900 grams. If someone left the *Rami* of all days until the 13th of *Zul Hijjah* he or she may do it in the sequence of days, and he will give *Dum* for the delay. And if he or she left all three *Jamarat* still he or she is bound to give only one *Dum*. This is like shaving one's head in *ihram* where there is one *Dum* for the whole head and 1/4th as well. It would be the case if he did not do *rami* of all days until the time was over, which is until sunset on the 13th.

To *Malikites* if he delays even one stone until nightfall, he can hit that one stone at night or next day and will give a *Dum*. And if he makes the *Qada* of *rami* of the 10th or 11th or 12th on the 13th before sunset he or she will still give a *Dum* as well. Also, if he or she did all three *Jamarat* but not in order he will give a *Dum*. One who makes someone his agent to do his *rami* will still give a *Dum*, or he has no sin, and the agent will give a second *Dum* if he or she delayed the *rami* of his client without any just cause.

According to *Shafites* and *Hanbalites*, if someone misses the *rami* of a *Jamrah* or more or a day or more as well, he can do it the next day or even on the 13th before sunset, because the *Prophet* allowed those who were arranging water and grass for their animals to do so. Then if someone leaves all days of *rami* or less, even if he left three stones of *Jamrah*, he may give *Dum*.

Staying at *Mina* the night between the 8th and 9th is *Sunnah* according to all of them, while staying at *Mina* at night in *Ayyamut Tashreeq* is also *Sunnah* according to *Hanafites* and *Wajib* according to *Malikites* and *Shafites*, but for those who have an acceptable excuse. But without reason, it will cost him or her *Dum* and to *Hanbalites* there are two views:

i. Nothing is there if he misses it;

ii. *Dum* is *Wajib* if he or she misses it, and as we said, *Tarteeb* (order) in *Rami* of *Jamarat Ul Aqabah* then *Zab'h*. Then the shave/trim is *Wajib* according to *Hanafites* and *Sunnah* according to *Jumhur*, and to do *Tawaf Ul Ifadah* after this is *Sunnah*, but to do this *Rami* before *Tawaf* is *Wajib*.

SHAVE/TRIM

The shave/trim in *Hajj* and *Umrah* is a *Ruk'n* according to *Shafites* and *Wajib* according to *Jumhur*.

Allah said:

Moreover, to take away their Tafath (22:29).

Ibni Umar said

It meant to shave and put on one's usual dress. Anas said that the Prophet came to Mina to Jamrah so he did Rami, then he came to his place in Mina and did Zab'h, then he said to the barber, "Take [shave]," and pointed to the right side of his head, then to the left, and then he started giving it to the people (Ahmad, Muslim, Abu Dawud).

Abu Hurairah said:

That the Prophet made a Dua,

"O Allah! Forgive those who shaved, they said, and those who trimmed," the Prophet said, "O Allah, forgive those who shaved," they said, and those who trimmed then the prophet said, "And those who trimmed" (Bukhari, Muslim).

Ibni Hibban narrated a *Hadith* that the *Prophet* said;

Anyone who shaved, for each fallen hair there will be a light on the day of resurrection. But for ladies it should only be a trim as the Prophet said (Dari Qutni, Abu Dawud from Ibni Abbas).

Imam Tirmizi related from *Aisha* that the *Prophet* forbade women to shave.

The *Shafites* say a man should trim a little from his beard and mustache as well. One who is totally bald must pass the razor, as the *Prophet* said:

Whatever I have commanded you, do it as much as you can (Bukhari, Muslim).

This process is *Wajib* for a bald man according to *Hanafites* and recommended according to others. Also, *Ibni Umar* said the same procedure may be adopted by the bald.

Shaving the whole head is recommended. But if he shaves 1/4th at least, his *Wajib* is done. But this is an unpopular practice, while a trim may be to the extent of 1/3 of the finger from all around according to *Malikites* and *Hanbalites*, and a little bit more than 1/3 of a finger from all around according to *Hanafites*, and according to *Shafites* at least to remove three hairs is *Fard*.

The shave/trim may be in *Ayyamun Nah'r* inside the limits of *Haram* according to *Hanafites*, but if he did it either after these days or outside *Haram*, then he may give *Dum*.

The *Malikites* said, if a man delays the shave/trim, there is no *Dum*, but if he goes to his town or city even if it is nearby, then there is a *Dum due* from him. The *Shafites* and the *Hanbalites* said, there is no *Dum* if he delayed it from its time, or he shaved/trimmed outside *Haram* limits or anywhere else. This delay is *Makrooh* and with this shave/trim, everything that was forbidden for him because of *Ihram* is allowed, except sex according to *Hanafites*, till he performed *Tawaf* while according to *Shafites* and *Hanbalites Nikah* is also not allowed yet. *Malikites* said sex, hunting, and perfume are also not allowed till he makes *Tawaf Ul Ifadah*.

ZAB'H

As we mentioned that *Zab'h* for one in *Hajji Ifrad* is *Sunnah*, but it is *Wajib* for one in *Tamattu* and *Qiran*. This *Zab'h* is thanks to *Allah* that He used his travel for *Hajj* in such a way that he performed *Umrah* also, for which he is bound to do *Zab'h*.

Allah said:

> *So, whosoever exploited his Hajj for "Umrah", so whatever is easy for him means "Had'y" [gift] sacrifice (2:196).*

The one who did it can eat from that also according to *Hanafites*, but not according to *Shafites,* if someone made intention for *Hajji Qiran*, but then he did not come to *Makkah*, and went straight to *Arafat*. According to *Hanafites* he dropped his *Umrah*, so his *Zab'h* is also dropped, but because of dropping his *Umrah*, he will give a *Dum* from which he cannot eat. He is bound for *Qada* of that *Umrah* also, as according to *Hanafites* when someone started in a *Naf'l Ibadah*, and then he broke it, then he is bound for its

Qada. While according to *Shafites* if he went back to *Meeqat* once again after performing the *Umrah* of *Hajji Tamattu*, then his *Zab'h* is dropped. Then according to *Jumhur* this *Zab'h* may be at *Mina* in *Ayyamun Nah'r* (10th, 11th, and 12th) after the *Rami* of *Aqabah* on 10th as the *Prophet* did it in such a way.

The *Shafites* said this is best to do it on the 10th, but the *Wujub's* time is when he or she put on *ihram* for *Hajj*. Then if someone did not find, or he could not do this sacrifice, he or she may fast ten days.

But how?

The *Hanafites* say, three days in the months of *Hajj* after that he put on *Ihram* for *Umrah* as

Allah said:

> *Then fasting for three days in Hajj (2:196).*

It means in the months of *Hajj*; the best way is to fast on the 7th, 8th, and 9th. To do it sequentially is not a requirement, but if he or she cannot do it until the 9th day has passed, then there is *Zab'h* only as the verse mentioned for it the time of *Hajj* if he did not find *Qurbani*, and seven days he or she will fast after *Ayyamut Tashreeq* whenever he or she wants to do, as

Allah said:

And seven (days) when he returned (free from Hajj) (2:196).

Of course, it will be after *Ayyamut Tashreeq*. Then there are three days one can fast before starting *Hajj*.

The *Malikites* say, in these three days and also in the seven days, the consistency is a *Shart* and the three days may be in *Hajj* days, but the last day of these three may be *Arafah* (the 9th), but if someone forgot it, then he or she may do it in *Mina* on the 11th, 12th, and 13th, but it is not allowed to fast these three days before starting *Hajj*; while he or she can fast seven days after *Hajj* is over.

According to *Shafites*, consistency is recommended. However, if someone cannot do the three days before the 10th, then he or she is bound to make its *Qada*, but must have an interval of four days between these three and the other seven as this interval was four days, the 10th, 11th, 12th, and 13th, so if he or she fasted ten days without interval, then three days are considered but not the seven others, so he or she may fast there 7 days again; but he or she cannot fast these three before *ihram* because fasting is physical *Ibadah*, which is not allowed before time. *Zab'h* is allowed before. He or she should complete the three days before *Arafah*, as fasting of *Arafah* for one in *Hajj* is *Makrooh* while the seven days he or she will fast when he or she arrives home back or if he or she stays at *Makkah*, he or she can fast there. According to *Hanbalites*, consistency in that fasting is not a must. Then a recommended time for the three days is in between his or her *Ihram* for *Hajj* and *Arafah* and the last day should be the 9th. It is also permissible to fast it when he or she puts on *Ihram* for *Umrah* as the *Hanafites* said. The recommended time for the seven days is when he or she returns home, while permissible time is after *Ayyamut Tashreeq* wherever he is. If someone misses the three days, he or she can make a *Qada* of that, even in three days of *Mina*. *Imam Bukhari* narrated from Umar and Aisha that fasting is not allowed in *Ayyamut*

Tashreeq, but for one who could not do *Qurbani*, that is allowed.

Allah said, *"Three days in Hajj"* and there are no other days of *Hajj* but only these *Ayyamut Tashreeq*. *Hanbalites* do not mean to separate these three days from the seven days; one can fast all ten together in sequence. The time for fasting is the time of *Qurbani* as well, as this fasting is a substitute to *Qurbani*.

TAWAF UL WIDA

This *Tawaf is Wajib* according to *Hanafites*, *Shafites* and *Hanbalites* and *Sunnah* according to *Malikites*. The details are given in the chapter on *Tawaf*.

SUNNAH OF *HAJJ* AND *UMRAH*

1. Bathing and putting perfume on the body or even on *Ihram*, but not according to *Malikites* as it remains after as well, but to use fragrance after that one makes intention is not allowed.

2. To say *Talbiyah* as much as one can, especially after prayer.

3. *Tawaf Ul Qudum* is *Sunnah* according to *Jumhur* but *Wajib* according to *Malikites*.

4. Two *Rakat* after *Tawaf* is *Sunnah* according to *Shafites* and *Hanbalites*, and *Wajib* according to *Hanafites* and *Malikites*.

5. Staying at *Mina* on the night of the 10th *Zul Hijjah* is *Sunnah*.

6. *Wuquf* at *Muzdalafah* at night is *Sunnah* according to *Hanafites*. The *Wajib* according to them is *Wuquf* after *Fajr*.

7. Staying at *Mina* on the night of the 11th and 12th and, if one wants, the 13th night as well, is *Sunnah* according to *Hanafites*.

8. To take a rest in *Muhassab* valley between *Mina* and *Makkah*, i.e., in *Kheif* is *Sunnah* according to *Hanafites* and *Hanbalites* and recommended according to *Shafites* and *Malikites*.

9. *Khutbahs* – These are three in number according to *Hanafites, Malikites,* and *Hanbalites*:

i. One on 7th of *Zul Hijjah* at *Makkah* after *Zuhr* prayer teaching the *Manasik* therein. It is only one *Khutbah*, not two parts. To *Jumhur*, this is the first *Khutbah*. *Ibni Umar* said, the *Prophet* taught people the *Manasik* before *Yaumut Tarwiyah* by one day, i.e., on 7th, but the first *Khutbah*, according to *Hanbalites* is the *Khutbah* at *Arafat* on 9th. If *Yaumut Tarwiyah* appeared on Friday then according to *Shafites* they may go out towards *Mina* before *Fajr*, as traveling after *Fajr* on Friday is not allowed near them. However, if the day of *Arafah* is Friday, then going out of *Mina* towards *Arafat* is allowed after *Fajr* because the *Prophet* did not pray at *Arafat* on Friday. However, according to *Hanbalites* on *Tarwiyah* (8th), if that is Friday, they can stay until Friday prayer, and they can even go out after *Fajr*.

ii. *Khutbah* of *Arafah* – This *Khutbah* is in two parts (two *Khutbahs*) like Friday and *Eid*, and then the *imam* will lead *Zuhr* and *Asr* prayer in *Zuhr* time.

iii. *Khutbah* on *Eid* day. This one is the third one according to *Shafites*, and second according to *Hanbalites* as *Rafi Ibni Amr Al Muzani* said,

"I saw the *Prophet* on a mule giving *Khutbah* at *Mina*." (*Abu Dawud*)

iv. *Khutbah* on 12th of *Zul Hijjah*. This is the 4th *Khutbah* according to *Shafites* and third according to *Jumhur* as *Abu Dawud* narrated from two men of *Banu Bakr* and *Dari Qutni* related it from *Sara Binti Nabhan* that the *Prophet* gave a *Khutbah* in the middle of *Ayyamut Tashreeq* in brief, according to *Malikites* and *Hanafites* the *Khutbahs* are three:

a) On 7th at *Makkah*

b) On 9th at *Arafat*

c) On 11th at *Mina*

Near *Hanbalites* there are three as well, but they are:

a) On 9th at *Arafat*

b) On 10th at *Mina*

c) On 11th at *Mina* as well

The *Shafites* said there are four *Khutbahs*:

a) On 7th at *Makkah*

b) On 9th at *Arafat*

c) On 10th at *Mina*

d) On 13th at *Mina* as well

RESTRICTIONS IN *IHRAM*

While someone makes intention for *Umrah* or *Hajj*, then certain things are prohibited that were permissible before that *Ihram* and this prohibition is until he or she shaves/trims. For these prohibitions, we shall say that its roots are four:

i. To wear any sewn clothing

ii. To clean one's body or to give it enjoyment

iii. Hunting

iv. Sexual relations with one's wife.

The first three cause a penalty, while the last one nullifies the *Hajj*. The details are:

1. **Wearing Sewn Clothes**: For men after *Ihram* it is forbidden to cover his head totally or partially. Even if the cover is not sewn, as the *Prophet* said regarding one who fell from his camel and he was in *Ihram*:

> *Don't cover his head. Indeed, he would be resurrected on the Day of Resurrection saying "Talbiyah (Bukhari, Muslim, Ahmad, Nisa'i, Ibni Majah)."*

However, if a cover is needed, then he can cover. But he must pay the *Fidyah* according to all. To carry something and put it on his head is *Makrooh* according to *Shafites*. Also, it is not allowed to wear a shirt, gown, trouser, or socks. But if he cannot find the needed slippers for *ihram,* he may cut his leather socks to beneath the ankles, according to *Hanafites* and *Malikites,* while he can use them without cutting them according to *Shafites* and *Hanbalites*. To wear a trousers or leather socks in need, *Imam Bukhari*, and *Imam Muslim* both narrated from *Ibni Abbas* that I heard the *Prophet* at *Arafat*, he was saying:

> *"Whosoever could not find slippers, he should wear leather socks, so whosoever could not find Izar he should wear trousers."*

However, this will cause him *Fidyah* according to *Hanafites* and *Malikites* as *Bukhari* and *Muslim* narrated from *Ibni Umar* that someone asked the *Prophet* what a *Muhrim* should wear? The *Prophet* said he may not wear a shirt, nor a turban, nor trousers, nor (sewn) cloaks, nor socks. However, one who cannot not find slippers should wear leather socks, and he may cut them beneath the ankles.

Shafites and *Hanbalites* said it is not needed to cut the socks as *Ibni Abbas* narrated. That *Hadith* is after the *Hadith* of *Ibni Umar* as the *Prophet* said it in *Arafat*, so it has abrogated the *hadith* of *Ibni Umar*, and when one did it, then there is no *Fidyah* due on him. Also, according to *Hanbalites*, there is no due *Fidyah* on one who wore a trouser in need. A shoe that covers the toes is allowed according to *Shafites*, but it is prohibited from tying the *Izar* with button or rope. But to put a knot to it is allowed according to *Shafites*, but not allowed for the upper cloak. But to put a knot to *Izar* is *Makrooh* according to *Hanafites*, but to put a *Himyan* (money belt) is allowed. Women may cover their entire body with a full dress except the face, as the Prophet said:

> *Women may not put on Niqab [face veil] nor put on gloves.*

But according to *Hanafites*, when there are men, then she may put on some cloth on but not touching her face, as *Abu Dawud* and *Ath'ram* narrated from *Aisha* that we used to do this when men were passing by. Also, this is allowed near others as well.

2. **<u>A Muhrim</u>** cannot put fragrance on his body nor his *ihram* according to *Hanafites, Shafites*, and *Malikites*, nor he can use any oil, scented or not. But he can use *Kuhl* (kohl) according to *Hanafites*. Near *Malikites*, he can use it if he needs it and if he used it without necessity, then he may pay *Fidyah*, according to *Hanafites, Malikites,* and *Shafites*. While according to *Shafites* if he puts on some fragrance forgetfully, or he was forced to use it, or he did not know that it was scented, then there is neither sin nor *Fidyah*. Near *Malikites*, he may not eat or drink something having fragrance if it is not cooked. Bathing is allowed according to *Hanafites, Shafites, Malikites* and *Hanbalites,* while according to *Hanbalites* using fragrance, even if he smelled it purposely, is prohibited, and he may pay the *Fidyah*.

Also, he cannot cut, trim or pluck a hair of his body, nor he can cut his nails. If someone in *Ihram* shaved his whole head or 1/4 of it, then he may give *Dum* according to *Hanafites* if he had an excuse then he will either fast, give *Sadaqah*, pay *Fidyah* or give *Dum*, and if he shaves less than 1/4 then he may give *Sadaqah*, and if he plucks his armpit, he may give *Dum*, and if he cuts the nails of one hand or one foot then he may give *Dum* as well, but in less than that there is *Sadaqah* if there is not just excuse. To *Malikites* in 10 nails there is *Sadaqah* of one full hand food/grain. According to *Shafites* and *Hanbalites* in one hair there is *Sadaqah* of one *Mudd* of food and in two hairs two *Mudds*, but in three or more there is *Dum*.

3. **NIKAH** is prohibited while one is in *ihram* according to *Jumhur* as *Imam Muslim* narrates that the *Prophet* said:

Muslim cannot do Nikah, nor his Nikah may be solemnized, nor he can propose.

That *Nikah* is *Batil* (void) while the proposal is *Makrooh*. But to *Hanafites*, it is allowed. They said that *Ibni Abbas* relates that the *Prophet* married *Maimunah*, and he was in *Ihram* (*Bukhari and Muslim*).

But *Jumhur*, said, that he married her when he was out of *ihram* as *Abu Rafi* relates (*Tirmizi*) and as *Maimunah* related (*Abu Dawud*).

Hanafites said in the *Hadith* of prohibition *Nikah* means sexual intercourse and that is *Haram*.

4. **HUNTING** is also not allowed for one in *Ihram*, nor he can advise or indicate another to hunt, whether the animal or bird is edible or not. However, if the animal is harmful, like a lion or a snake, he may kill it for protection, and he can hunt water animal like fish, and he can slaughter domestic animals as well according to *Hanafites*. Even if something is hunted for *Muhrim* it is not allowed according to *Jumhur* as *Imam Ahmad, Imam Bukhari* and *Imam Muslim* narrated from *Sa'b Ibni Ju'thamah* that the *Prophet* was in *Waddan* or *Abwa* (places),

and a wild donkey was brought to him, but he returned it, saying,

"We are in Ihram."

Also, a *Muhrim* cannot kill lice as they are born of his body/hair, nor he can kill a locust, and if a *Muhrim* slaughters a hunted animal or bird, then that is *Haram*. Then if something is hunted for a *Muhrim,* is allowed for *Muhrims* to eat from as *Bukhari* and *Muslim* narrated from *Abu Qatadah* when he hunted a wild donkey and his friends were in *Ihram*, the *Prophet* asked has anyone asked him or indicated to, and they said,

"No."

The *Prophet* said,

"Then eat,"

but this is not allowed according to *Jumhur*, but the one which is hunted by one who is not in *Ihram* and then he presented it to *Muhrim* then that is allowed according to all, as *Abu Dawud*, *Nisa'i* and *Tirmizi* narrated the *Prophet* said,

> *"The hunt of the earth is allowed for you (O Muhrims) if you have not hunted and not hunted for you."*

However, the hunted one for a specific *Muhrim* is allowed for another *Muhrim* according to *Uthman*, but not according to *Ali*.

To hunt a non-edible animal or bird is allowed according to *Shafites* and *Hanbalites*, but not according to *Hanafites* and *Malikites*, but only if the animal is dangerous. Moreover, if a *Muhrim* falls prey to necessity, where eating *Haram* is allowed, and he found an edible hunted animal and another one dead, he may eat from the dead one according to *Malikites* and *Hanbalites* and eat from the hunted one according to *Shafites*. This is allowed in *Ihram* if he washes his hair, but according to *Malikites* and *Hanbalites* with water only, while *Hanafites* and *Shafites* allowed with something, which takes out the dirt, but has no fragrance. To look into a mirror is *Makrooh* according to *Malikites* and *Hanbalites* and allowed according to *Hanafites* and *Shafites*. Also, fastening a money belt is allowed. The *Muhrim* should try not to speak a lot, but if that is good then it is ok.

COMPENSATION FOR *JINAYAT*

Jenayat in this regard is something that is prohibited because of *Haram* or because of *Ihram*.

(1) *Jenayat* Because of *Ihram:* If he did not do that which is required in *Hajj* and *Umrah* or he did something which is prohibited in *Ihram* or even if he did it forgetfully or ignorantly or negligently or even he was forced to do it, if the *Muhrim* is not an adult, and he did something that is prohibited then there is nothing due on him according to *Jumhur*. The *Shafites* said, if the minor did something that is prohibited, then he may pay the *Fidyah* and will make a *Qada* if his *Hajj* is broken. This is one saying of them. Yes, if he performed sexual intercourse, his *Hajj* is *Fasid* near all. But there is no *Qada* due on him according to *Hanafites* and *Malikites*, and there is *Qada* in one saying of both *Shafites* and *Hanbalites*.

(2) *Jenayat* Regarding *Haram* like cutting off its tree even though if he is not in the form of *Ihram* or even he did the same ignorantly, forgetfully, negligently, or he was forced to do the same, it costs him *Daman* (compensation by *Fidyah*). Then in the former case, i.e., *Jinayah* because of *ihram* causes different types to compensate this violation. So, if he puts on a sewn garment or covers his head for one day, he may slaughter a lamb, and if he shaved 1/4 of his head or 1/4 of his beard, this is the case. But if he dressed for less than a day or shaved less than 1/4, then there is *Sadaqah* due from him. If he cuts all his nails or the nails of both hands or both feet or one hand or one foot in one sitting, he is bound to slaughter a lamb, and if he cuts the nails of both hands in one sitting and the nails of his feet in another sitting, then he may slaughter two. However, if he cuts less than five nails, then a *Sadaqah* is due on him.

If the *Muhrim* puts fragrance over one complete part of his body or on the whole body, he may slaughter a lamb, and if he puts fragrance on his *Ihram* and keeps it on his body for the whole day, again he may slaughter a lamb, if he put *Khidab* (henna) on his hand, head or beard then he may slaughter a lamb. But if he did any of these aforementioned because for some good reason, then he has the option to slaughter a lamb or to fast three days or to feed six poor people, as *Allah* recommended. This is according to *Hanafites*, while *Jumhur* said, whosoever puts on a sewn garment while he was *Muhrim* or shaved or cut his nails or put on fragrance he did it knowingly or unknowingly, did it without any excuse or because of it has an option of one of the aforesaid three things, i.e., slaughter or fasting or feeding, while this option is only in case of a just excuse according to *Abu Hanifa*.

This *Fidyah* is becoming binding on one who cut even three hairs only but constantly according to *Shafites* and on one who cut more than two hairs or more than two nails according to *Hanbalites*. If a *Muhrim* shaved the head of a *Halal* (who is not in *ihram*) then there is a *Fidyah* due on him according to *Hanafites* but not according to *Jumhur*, and if a *Halal* one or another *Muhrim* shaved the head of a *Muhrim* with his permission, then the shaved one may pay the *Fidyah*. However, if he was shaved by force or when he was sleeping, then he may pay the same according to *Hanafites*, but not according to *Malikites* and *Hanbalites*, while *Shafites* have the like of the two sayings.

In case of sexual intercourse before *Arafah*, even if that happened forgetfully or by force or even if she was sleeping, the *Hajj* became *Fasid*. He may slaughter a lamb and must carry on his *Hajj* and must make its *Qada* s soon as he can even if his *Hajj* was a *Naf'l* one. If someone performs sexual intercourse after *Wuquf* at *Arafah*, but before the first *Tahallul* his *Hajj* became *Fasid* according to *Jumhur*, but not according to *Hanafites*. He may slaughter a *Badnah* (cow or camel) according to *Hanafites* and if he did the same again, now he may slaughter a lamb as he did it now in such an *ihram* that is already disgraced while according to *Shafites* and *Hanbalites* he may slaughter a *Badnah* if he had sex before the first *Tahallul*. If he could not find then he may slaughter seven lambs, and if he cannot find any then he may donate the price of a *Badnah* to feed the poor, and if he cannot do that then he may fast one day for each *Mudd* of that food, but if that happened after the first *Tahallul* and before the second one or he had it after that it became *Fasid* then he may slaughter a lamb. To *Malikites* a *Hadi* (camel, then cow, then lamb) is due in case of sexual intercourse or discharge (not including *Ihtilam*) that is before *Wuquf* or after *Wuquf* and before *Rami* of *Jamrat Ul Aqabah* and before *Tawaf Ul Ifadah*.

In case of the *Muqaddimat* of sexual touch or amorous kiss, if there is discharge, there is a lamb to be slaughtered. The same would be the case if he discharged *Mazi* (a fluid that comes out of the penis when one is aroused). Also, a second incident of sexual intercourse after he has done another one already and a case of sex between the two *Tahallul*, any discharge (but not as *Ihtilam*) makes the *Hajj Fasid* according to *Malikites*.

SKETCH

1. Putting on a sewn garment or covering his head without excuse; or a lady covering her face.	LAMB MAY BE SLAUGHTERED.
2. Removing hair of any part of the body.	i. If that is 1/4 of the head then he may slaughter a lamb; and if less than that then he may give *Sadaqah* according to Hanafites ii. Near *Shafites* and *Hanbalites* a lamb is due if he removed three or more hairs, otherwise he may give *Sadaqah* to feed the poor according to *Hanbalites* and to give one *Mudd* for one hair and two for two according to *Shafites*. iii. Near *Malikites* if he removed more than ten hairs, he may slaughter a lamb, otherwise

	he may give *Sadaqah* of one full hand of food.
3. Cutting Nails	i. Near *Hanafites* there is lamb for cutting of the nails of one hand or one foot, otherwise *Sadaqah*. ii. Near *Jumhur*, the same as in the case of hair.
4. Using Fragrance	MUST SLAUGHTER A LAMB.

5. Hunting or Indicating to hunt.	i.	To pay its equal or to pay its price or to fast one day for each *Mudd* of its price of equivalent food.
	ii.	To pay the price in case of a *Hadi* to be slaughtered or to give food equal to the price or to fast one day for even 1/2 *Sa*.
6. Cutting of the green of *Haram*.	i.	There is nothing according to *Malikites*.
	ii.	To pay the price according to *Hanafites*.
	iii.	To slaughter a lamb or a cow, depending on how the size of the tree, according to *Shafites* and *Hanbalites* and to pay the price if that is a little.

7. Sexual Intercourse and Its *Muqaddimat*	In the case of sexual intercourse, the *Hajj* has become *Fasid* according to all schools while that is *Fasid* with discharge only (but not as *Ihtilam*) according to Malikites, so *Qada* is due when it became "Fasid." He may slaughter a *Badnah* according to *Shafites* and *Hanbalites*, a *Hadi* (camel or cow or lamb) according to *Malikites*, and slaughter a *Badnah* according to *Hanafites* if that is after *Wuquf* and a lamb if it is before it. There is no *Fidyah* on a sleeping or a forced woman if that is done to her according to *Ahmad*, while according to *Shafites* if someone did the *Muqaddimat* of an amorous kiss, touch, or hug forgetfully then nothing is due from him; it is also the case if he did Sexual Intercourse forgetfully or not realizing that this is prohibited or if a woman is forced; nothing is due on them nor does this make their *Hajj Fasid* according to them.

> NOTE: Whatsoever causes one *Dum* to one who is in *Ifrad* or *Tamattu* will cause two to one in *Qiran* according to *Hanafites*. To *Jumhur*, *Qiran* is like *Ifrad* in *Jenayat*, so if he performs Sexual Intercourse he will slaughter one *Badnah* and not two, but he may slaughter the lamb for *Qiran* as well.

MISSING A *WAJIB* AND ITS COMPENSATION

Near *Hanafites*, as we said, that the mandatory in *Tawaf* is four rounds. If someone has missed three rounds, the *Tawaf* is done, but he has to compensate the missing three as under:

(1) In the case of *Tawaf Ul Qudum*, if he has missed four rounds, his *Sunnah* is not done, but nothing is there on him, but if gives *Sadaqah*. In the case of *Tawaf Uz Ziyarat*, if he missed four, his *Fard* is not done, and he is *Muhrim* till he does it. But if he missed three rounds or less than three, then he may slaughter a lamb. If he missed four rounds of *Tawaf Ul Wida* he may slaughter a lamb while in missing of less than four, he may give some *Sadaqah*.

(2) But if someone made his *Tawaf Ul Qudum* and was without *wudu*, he may give *Sadaqah*, and if he was *Junub* (impure) he may slaughter a lamb. If he made *Tawaf Uz Ziyarat* without *Wudu*, he may slaughter a lamb and if he was in the form of *Junabat* then he may slaughter a *Badnah*. But it is good for him to remake it in purity and *wudu*, and then his slaughter is dropped. If he did *Tawaf Ul Wida* without *Wudu* he may give *Sadaqah*, and if he did it in the form of *Junabat*, then he may slaughter a lamb.

(3) If someone did T*awaf* and 1/4 of an organ of *Aurah* was open, he may remake it. If he did not do so until he went out of *Makkah*, then he may slaughter a lamb.

(4) Missing four or more rounds of *Sai* costs one lamb, while less costs *Sadaqah*.

(5) If one left *Arafat* before sunset, he may slaughter a lamb. But if he returned to *Arafat* before sunset and stayed there until sunset, then the lamb is not required.

(6) Missing *Wuquf* at *Muzdalafah* costs one lamb.

(7) Missing the *Jamarat* of all days or of one day complete or of *Jamarat Ul Aqabah* on 10th costs one lamb. However, missing of only one of the three *Jamarat* or two of the three one day will cost *Sadaqah*.

(8) If someone delayed *Tawaf Uz Ziyarat* or shaving head until *Ayyamun Nah'r* passed, a lamb is due from him according to *Abu Hanifa*, but nothing is there according to *Abu Yusuf* and *Muhammad*.

To *Malikites*, the compensation will be *Fidyah*, same as a hunted animal or bird or a *Hadi*. Then the *Hadi* is required in five cases:

i. If he has missed a *Wajib* like a *Talbiyah*, *Tawaf Ul Qudum*, *Rami*, a stay at *Muzdalafah* or in *Mina*.

ii. The expiation for sexual intercourse or for kissing or for *Mazi* he discharged when looking at someone with desire.

The *Shafites* said the compensation will be a *Dum* if –

i. He missed *Ihram* from *Meeqat*.

ii. He missed staying at night at *Muzdalafah* or at *Mina*.

iii. He missed *Tawaf Ul Wida*.

However, if he had sex, then he may slaughter a camel. If he cannot not find one, a cow will suffice. If he cannot find a cow, then he may slaughter seven lambs; and if he cannot find these, then he may give food equal to the price of a camel. If he cannot not do this, then he may fast one day for each *Mudd*.

In the case of been stopped from *Hajj*, a lamb is due, and if he cannot find then food equal to its price and if not then fasting. In the case of removing three hairs or cutting three nails constantly, he has the option to slaughter a lamb or to feed six poor people or fast for three days. It is the case if he used fragrance or wore sewn garments or discharged himself in any way other than sexual intercourse or he kissed or touched with desire. In the event of a shave, the *Fidyah* is due even though if he did it forgetfully, or he did not know that this is forbidden.

To *Hanbalites* if he dressed or put fragrance or covered his head, removed more than two hairs or more than two nails or kissed or touched with desire. He may slaughter a lamb or fast for three days or feed six poor people. In the case of missing a *Wajib* or stoppage from *Hajj*, he may slaughter and if he cannot, due to poverty, then he may fast ten days. In case of poverty when he could not slaughter a lamb of *Tamattu* or *Qiran* he may fast three days in *Hajj* and seven days after that. However, if he did not fast the three days in *Ayyamun Nah'r* then he may fast all ten days after that, but he may slaughter a lamb also.

In case of sexual intercourse or discharge in any way or touching with desire there is a *Badnah* due from him or a fast of ten days. Then the slaughter of *Hajj* must be in *Haram* according to all schools. However, the *Fidyah* that is due for anything other than hunting and sex could be done anywhere anytime according to *Malikites* and according to *Shafites*; in case of stoppage from *Hajj* he can slaughter anywhere. Also, the slaughter in *Tamattu* one can even do before *ihram* for *Hajj*. The *Hanbalites* said, the *Fidyah* for covering the head, wearing a sewn garment, using fragrance or doing any forbidden act other than hunting could be anywhere.

MISSING *HAJJ* AFTER *IHRAM*

The *Hanafites* said whosoever missed the *Hajj*, and he had done *Ihram* for that, may make *Umrah*. Moreover, he will remake his *Hajj* the following year, i.e., as soon as he can, and there is no *Dum* due from him. However, according to *Jumhur* he will do *Umrah* and will make *Qada* the following year. However, at the time of *Qada* he will slaughter a lamb as that is in the *Hadith* by *Bukhari*, the *Prophet* said as *Ibni Abbas* relates:

> *Whosoever missed Arafat he has missed the Hajj he should make himself Halal by Umrah and Hajj is due on him the following year (Dari Qutni).*

This *Qada* will be the way he missed it so a *Qarin* will do *Qiran* and will slaughter two lambs, one for *Qiran* and another one for what he missed. This is according to *Jumhur* while to *Abu Hanifa* he has done an *Umrah*, but has not become *Halal* until he makes *Tawaf* and *Sai* for *Hajj*, so he will slaughter one lamb only.

If a woman's menses started after *Ihram* for *Umrah* in her *Hajj* trip, she may change her intention to *Hajj* and her *Umrah* is dropped according to *Abu Hanifa*. However, according to *Jumhur*, she became *Qarinah* by doing so, and if her menses started while she was in *Hajj*, and she was to leave, But still she has not done her *Tawaf Ul Hajj* she may bathe and makes *Tawaf* and *Sai* and may slaughter a *Badnah* according to *Hanafites*.

IHSAR OR CEASURE FROM *HAJJ*

Ihsar is a ceasure from both the *Arkan* of *Hajj* according to *Hanafites* and that is a censure from the completion of *Hajj* or *Umrah*. This ceasure could be due to an enemy, sickness, loss of all of one's money, incarceration, breakage, or paralysis, even if he was at *Makkah*. However, according to *Jumhur*, *Ihsar* is a ceasure by the enemy. Otherwise, he may wait until he is better, and go to *Makkah* and do *Umrah*, and then he will make a *Qada* of his *Hajj*. If he was not at *Makkah*, then he is *Muhrim* till he makes *Tawaf*. If at the time of *ihram,* he put a condition to become *Halal*, if he got stuck due to some reason like as the *Prophet* told *Duba'a*, daughter of *Zubair* to say

> *"My place of becoming Halal is where you ceased me."*

This was when she was sick, but other reasons could also be included. However, according to *Hanafites* and *Shafites* still *Dum* is due on him while according to *Hanbalites* there is nothing due on him neither *Dum* nor *Qada*.

The place for slaughter in *Hajj* is *Haram* according to all, but *Malik* said if he brought his animal with him from outside, and it was with him in *Arafah* also, and he was slaughtering at *Yaumun Nah'r*, then it may be at *Mina* only. However, the *Dum* which became due in *Ihsar* is where he is ceased according to *Jumhur*, but that is also *Haram* according to *Hanafites*. This slaughter could be before *Yaumun Nah'r* according to *Abu Hanifa*, but *Abu Yusuf* and *Muhammad* said it must be on *Yaumun Nah'r*, and there is no *Dum* on a ceased one according to *Malikites*.

Then according to *Hanafites*, this *Qada* may be the way he missed it so a *Mufrid* will do *Ifrad* and a *Qarin* will do *Qiran*. However, he will do an extra *Umrah* with that also as he was supposed to become *Halal* with *Umrah* but he could not, so that is also due on him. However, one who is ceased from *Umrah*, he will make the *Qada* of *Umrah* alone.

To *Malikites Fard Hajj* is not dropped in case of ceasing even if he has become *Halal* with an *Umrah*, but in a *Naf'l* one he must make the

Qada if he was ceased due to sickness or incarceration. However, if it was illegal, or an enemy ceased him, then there is no *Qada* due from him.

The *Shafites* said in the case of *Nafl* there is no *Qada* due on him. However, in the event of a *Fard Hajj* if this was the very first year the *Hajj* has become *Fard* on him, then if he could do it next in future, he will. However, if it was after that first year when it became *Fard* on him, then he is bound to do it. It is the case according to *Hanbalites* also.

TRIP TO *MEDINA*

Going to *Madinah* is not part of *Hajj*. When someone is going to *Madinah* should he go with the intention of the *Masjid* or with the intention of *Ziyarah* of the *Prophet* or both?

Some scholars are of the view that to travel for any place with the intention of reward other than the three *Masajid* is not allowed. Some others said that the *Hadith* regarding *Masajid* that going to any *Masjid* with the intention of extra reward is not permitted, only as an additional reward of *Ibadah* is there for these three *Masajid*. People who are going to seek knowledge of *Deen* and have the intention of reward as well would be rewarded. Regarding the sacred grave of the *Prophet*, there are a few *Ahadith*, and none of them are fake; at most, some could be *Daeef*. When one *hadith* is narrated through more than one-way, and all its narrations are *Daeef*, it elevates to the level of *Hasan Lighairihi*, which is a type of *Maqbool Hadith*.

The *Ahadith* are:

Whosoever visited my grave; my intercession is due for him (Dari Qutni, Ibni Khuzaimah).

"Whosoever came to me visiting, nothing but my Ziyarah has brought him forth, then that is due on Allah that I will be his intercessor on the Day of Judgment (Ibnus Sakan)."

Whosoever performed Hajj and then visited my grave after my death, he is as if he has visited me in my lifetime (Dari Qutni).

Whosoever did Hajj, *and he did not visit me, he has treated me rudely (Dari Qutni, Ibni Hibban, Ibni Adi).*

Whosoever visited me after my death, so he is if he has visited me in my lifetime (Dari Qutni, Bayhaqi, Ibn Adi, Abu Yala).

To us one may make the intention of the *Masjid* and *Ziyarat*, both to get out of differences. Then he may say *Salam* to the *Prophet* then to *Abu Bakr* then to *Umar*. He may visit *Masjid-I-*

Quba the first ever *Masjid* of *Islam* built by the *Prophet* at the time of *Hijra*.

The *Prophet* said:

One prayer in Masjid I Quba is like an Umrah (Tirmizi).

Moreover, *Ibni Umar* said;

The Prophet used to go to Quba on foot and ride and to pray their two Rakat (Bukhari and Muslim).

It is in *Hadith* that the *Prophet* used to come to *Masjid-I-Quba* every Saturday. Also, it is *Sunnah* to go to *Jannat Ul Baqee*, the cemetery close to the *Masjid* where the *Sahabah*, the family of the *Prophet*, and other pious people are buried. The *Prophet* used to go there, sometimes even at night to visit the *Shuhada* of *Uhud*, as the *Prophet* used to go there as well. This is also *Sunnah*. Other places have historical significance, like *Masjid Ul Qiblatain* or *Masajid-I-Saba*.

BOOKS BY *QAZI FAZL ULLAH*

Qazi Fazl Ullah has written other books. Below is a short list with summaries.

FIQH KEE TAREEKH WA IRTIQA (URDU)

Islam is *Deen* (religion) and is a complete code of life. Its laws are of two types, textual and deduced, but how the text is interpreted and how laws are deduced therefrom is called *"Jurisprudence"* and the laws are called *Fiqh*, and how this *Fiqh* got developed and compiled. This book gives the details about its stages of development.

MOHAMMADUR RASOOLULLAH (URDU)

The biography of the *Prophet Muhammad* was preserved from day one by his blessed companions. Then scholars and historians have written books in this regard in different times, both concise and detailed. This book on the biography of *Prophet Muhammad* is an excellent balance of concise and detailed, as a concise a book sometimes misses things, and people do not have time to read and understand too detailed a book. Another important feature of this book is that almost with every important part of the *Prophet's* biography, the relevant part of the *Holy Quran* has been quoted, which illustrates that the *Prophet's* life was the practical shape of the *Holy Book*.

SARMAYA DARANA NIZAM ISHTIRAKIYAT AUR ISLAM (URDU)

Humans, throughout their history, have thought ahead and planned their economics and economical needs. They created systems for these purposes. The three systems most widely practiced in history are capitalism, communism, and *Islam*. This book is a comparative study of these 3 economical systems and it proves that the *Islamic* system bestowed upon us by the Creator is the best one with regard to justice and no room for exploitation.

DAWAT O JIHAD (URDU)

The basic duty of every *Prophet* and his followers was and is to call the people towards *Allah* in a peaceful, attractive, and convincing way, and wherever and whenever they encounter resistance and hindrances in this regard, they must remove these hindrances. At times, this leads to fights, as when the conspiracy is big and the opponents try to take away their fundamental rights, so they have the right to defend it but how, when, and where? In this book, it is mentioned that *Islam* teaches us to convey, convince, and convert, but not to coerce. This book is an answer to anti-*Islamic* propaganda, especially about the concept of *Jihad* in *Islam*.

ISLAM AUR SIYASAT (URDU)

Islam and Politics—as it is known from the title that this book discusses *Islamic* political system, because *Islam* is *Deen*, meaning a complete code of life and not a set of a few rituals. It has its own system for state and government. So, wherever *Muslims* are in power, if they will implement this system, they meet the needs of everyone, regardless of color, caste, or religion. *Islam* covers the details, such as how to elect a government, and how to run the state to provide peace and justice to all.

RIYASATI ISLAMI KA TASWWAR (URDU)

The title means the concept of an *Islamic* state, and *"concept"* means its conduct. In this book, it is mentioned how and why a state and government is needed, and how that state and government may be and should be run. The Creator *Allah* the Almighty knows all our needs, necessities, qualities and shortcomings, so the system he has given is the only system that can ensure people's security and safety and can provide them peace and justice, making the state a welfare state.

USOOLUT - TAFSEER (ARABIC)

Every branch of science has its own rules, principles and methodologies, which provide guidelines for explaining it and how to interpret it, so this methodology is a circle or limits one may keep himself confines to, so he will not get lost or go astray.

This book covers the explanation of the *Holy Quran*, the last and final book of *Allah*. The book of *Allah* is the basic source of *Islam* and *Islamic* law, so its explanation requires certain rules to be followed in its explanation, so one may not be unbridled and without restraint, otherwise he will put his faith in danger.

DIRAYATUR RIWAYAH (ARABIC)

Hadith (sayings, actions and sanctions) of *Prophet Muhammad* is the second fundamental source of *Islam* and *Islamic* laws and also it is the interpretation of the *Holy Quran*. The companions of the *Prophet Muhammad* have preserved them in their memories and in their scriptures and the second and third generation took it from them and preserved them as well. Later on, when there was a fear of perversion, then these *Ahadith* were compiled officially and later on, the authentic scholars gathered them together in various books. Furthermore, critics compiled a biography of all these narrators and put certain rules about how a *Hadith* could be accepted. This book includes all these details.

HUJJIYATI HADITH (URDU)

This book is regarding the authenticity of *Hadith* of the *Prophet*, as there is a baseless propaganda that *Hadith* were not written in the time of the *Prophet*, but later on, making them unreliable. This is wrong, as *Sahaba* used to write *Ahadith* and sometimes the *Prophet* himself used to order them to write. But they trusted their memory more than writing. Official compilation took place later on, when *Muslim* rulers became aware of the weakness of people's memories and the loss of those individuals writing. This book provides all these details and makes it clear that *Hadith* is *Wahi* (Revelation) and source of *Islamic Shariah* (Law).

FUNDAMENTALISM, SECULARISM AUR ISLAM (URDU)

Propaganda is being spread either because of ignorance or with mala fide intention that *Islam* is fundamentalism.

Fundamentalism was a term used for Christianity when it blocked the ways of scientific research, invention and development, and some people wanted to adopt it as a basic guideline for states and government. So those who were with research and development branded that as fundamentalism. But *Islam* does not stop or block progress and research; rather, it encourages it and even orders scholars to go ahead and do research, as discussed in this book.

AL IJTIHADU WAT TAQLEED (URDU)

Humans are social and intellectual animals. They have all the same needs as animals, but they are distinct from them because of their intellect as they are looking for their ease, to do a little and get a lot. For this purpose, some intellectuals invent things and others follow them. Then as they are bound to obey the *Deen* of *Allah*, there are other intellectuals who deduce laws from its fundamental sources: the *Quran* and the *Sunnah*, and the less intellectuals follow them, as they should. This is the only intellectual and reasonable way. This book explains this issue and its importance.

MUSALMAN AURAT (URDU)

Allah created the world. He created humans and made them men and women. He gave different qualities to both genders for the smooth running of this life to depend upon each other, but as humans they are equal. Some women made history and they did memorable work that many men could not have done. This small book mentions some of the great work of some great women, particularly *Muslim* women, to make it clear that *Islam* deeply respects women and appreciates their contributions to society.

ASMATI RASOOL OR ZAWAJI AAISHA (URDU)

This world is a combination of opposites and some people have been given a great status. The messengers of *Allah* are the chosen and beloved of *Allah*. He made them and built them up for himself and his work. They are the most respected and honored people, and they must be given respect, as any disgrace to them can harm the feelings and sentiments of their followers, which can cause trouble. In this book this issue is discussed, as well as a misconception about the *Prophet's* marriage to *Aaisha*; namely, that she was minor at that time. Academically and research fully, this book corrects this misconception.

AL FARA'ID FIL AQA'ID (ARABIC)

Aqeedah and *Aqa'id* means faith and beliefs, respectively, and they are the base of *Deen*. Certain beliefs are the contents of *Iman*. What is important for a *Muslim* to believe? These are detailed in this concise book. Some *Muslim* sects have misconstrued some of these beliefs, so the book mentions that as well and makes the right faith clear.

QAWA'IDUT - TAJWEED (ARABIC)

One of the basic duties of the *Prophet* was to teach his followers how to recite the holy book properly. His *Sahabah* learnt it from him and then this became a specific science in future generations. They not only taught their students the proper way of recitation, they also wrote books about it. This science is called *Tajweed*, which literally means to make good, but in this science, it means to recite good. This book prescribes the basic rules for *Tajweed* as proper pronunciation not only makes the words and sounds good but also helps in giving the proper meaning of the word.

AL QAWA'IDUL FIQHIYAH (ARABIC)

Islam is *Deen* and a complete system and code of life. For each and every aspect of life there are rules and laws in *Islam*. Some of these rules are in text of the *Quran* and the *Sunnah*, while some others are deduced therefrom. For deduction, the authentic jurists have laid down rules of deduction and the qualities required for themselves.

Then, after deduction, they have found some commonalities in different laws in different chapters, so they laid down a common rule for that and these rules called *Al Qawa'idul - Fiqhiyah*, or legal maxims, which make the study of *Fiqh* easy and understandable. This book includes some known and famous legal maxims in all four schools of jurisprudence.

AL JIHAD FIL ISLAM (ARABIC)

Jihad is a very important issue in *Islam*; to defend life, property, honor and faith is not only a well-known right in each and every culture but also a duty in *Islam*, but how and when? This book is written on this subject; and as this issue is quite controversial, this is a reasonable answer to these questions in the light of the *Quran* and *Sunnah*.

MAULANA UBAIDULLAH SINDHI (URDU)

Maulana Ubaidullah Sindhi, originally from a *Sikh* family, accepted *Islam* when he was a teenager. He studied *Deen* in the proper and traditional way, then joined the freedom movement. He went through a lot of difficulties, and lived in exile for 24 years. As a revolutionary leader, he is controversial and many people wrote against him as well as for him. This book describes his personality, struggle, and thoughts to know who he was and how he was.

ASMATI RASOOL AND KHATMI NUBUWWAT (URDU)

Asmati Rasool and *Khatmi Nubuwwat* are reasonable and logical. This book consists of two parts. The defense of the *Prophet* and that of him being the last and final *Prophet* of *Allah* is a reasonable and logical thing, as *Allah* sent messengers in different times to different areas and different nations, and when they worked in their respected times in those areas, *Allah* sent the *Prophet Muhammad* to the entire world to combine their work and bring humanity together on the same theme, subject and faith that all those earlier messengers were sent for. This book is a concise, detailed and logical interpretation of this finality.

SAYYIDAH AAISHA'S AGE AT MARRIAGE (ENGLISH)

Islam is a Natural *Deen* or *Deen* of Nature. This is a balanced *Deen* providing a comprehensive justice system, and the *Holy Prophet* is the perfect role model as a perfect human. His words, actions, and sanctions are the proper interpretation of the *Holy Quran* and the second fundamental source of laws in *Islam*. There is a commonly held belief, especially among critics of *Islam*, that the *Prophet* married *Aaisha* when she was only nine years of age. In this book, all the details about this issue is given that how this word *Tis'aa* (which means nine) happened there and what the real story is to counter the false accounts and correct the record.

JIHAD IN ISLAM : WHY, HOW, AND WHEN? (ENGLISH)

Jihad as a word in *Arabic* means struggle or striving hard, especially for a noble cause, while as a term in *Islam*, it specifically means to fight in the path/cause of *Allah*. But when does this fight happen? When it is inevitable and unavoidable as the very integrity of a state, the lives of its citizens or the very ideology is facing a big danger. But a very baseless smear campaign is going on against *Jihad* and it is branded as a synonym to terrorism, so this book is a must to make the true concept of *Jihad* clear and counter the propaganda.

SHARIA AND POLITICS (ENGLISH)

Islam is *Deen* and *Deen* means a complete system and a perfect code of life as this is given by the very creator of the worlds, who knows all about his creatures, their qualities and their shortcomings, and can provide a perfect solution to their problems. But unfortunately, some people have been doing wrong in the name of *Khalafat* and presenting their wrong idea as the *Islamic* political system, so there was great need of a book that can present the proper shape of an *Islamic* state and *Islamic* political system given by the Creator; when executed properly, it is actually a mercy and blessing for the creatures. This book explains this concept clearly.

HAJJ & UMRAH IN ALL FOUR SCHOOLS OF JURISPRUDENCE (ENGLISH)

Hajj (pilgrimage to *Mecca*) is one of the Five Pillars of *Islam* and a very important but a complicated type of *Ibadah* (worship) as *Muslims* from all around the world get together to perform it together. They follow the interpretation of their *Imams* (jurists), sometimes they look at others when they do not perform a specific virtue the way they do, then they think they are doing wrong, which is not so, but all of them are performing correctly according to the interpretation of their *Imams*. This book gives all these details in sequence according to all four *Imams* the *Muslim Ummah* follows.

MOON SIGHTING, SALATUL TARAWEEH AND SALATUL WITR (ENGLISH)

The *Islamic* Calendar is lunar-based. It's different *Ibadaat* time is based on moon-sighting; the lunar month starts with the new moon. Even though astronomy tells us what day the moon will be born (i.e., new) with perfect accuracy, discerning on which day it will be visible in a specific area is still not accurate. That is why differences in opinion happen all over the world, and should we to go by the calendar or by a sighting?

Also, at *Ramadan*, which is the most important month in *Islam* as a mandatory *Ibadah*, fasting is mandatory as well, but there is an extra, highly recommended *Ibadah*, the *Taraweeh*, but how many *Rakat* should we pray? *Muslims* differ about this. Another important *Ibadah* is *Salat Ul Witr*. We use this prayer all year, but during *Ramadan* this is prayed in *Jama'at* and different *Imams* have different opinions regarding the number of *Rakats* and its procedure. So, this book gives all the details about these three important issues.

SCIENCE OF HADITH (ENGLISH)

Hadith is the second fundamental source of *Islamic* law. They are the words, actions and sanctions of the *Holy Prophet*. To record all these in memory and writing, to compile it and to record the biography of those narrators who did this great job and this is considered as a miracle of the *Prophet*. But the enemies of *Islam* used to create doubts in this regard. This book is written on this subject, and it is enough an answer to all the objections that people made from different angles.

ABOUT THE AUTHOR

Qazi Fazl Ullah is an American philosopher, linguist, and author. He is *Fazil Wafaqul Madaris* where he studied *Arabic* grammar, *Arabic* literature, *Fiqh*, jurisprudence, logic, philosophy, *Ilmul Kalam, Seerah, Tafseer, Hadith,* and *Islamic* history. He studied at *Peshawar University* and *Islamic University Islamabad* in *Pakistan* and specialized in law, economics, and political science. He has taught all these subjects in *Pakistan* and the United States at different institutions. He was elected as a *National Assembly Parliamentarian* in *Pakistan*. He worked in underserved areas to provide jobs, build infrastructure, schools, museums, public health facilities, and increase communication technologies as the chair of the *Social Action Board*. He has traveled extensively throughout the Middle East, North Africa, Europe, South East Asia, North and Central America. He has given seminars in various parts of the world in these subjects. He speaks and has given lectures and seminars in *Urdu, Pashto, Farsi,* English, and *Arabic*. He has published works in *Pashto, Urdu,*

Arabic, and English internationally. He has given the complete *Tafsir Ul Quran* in *Pashto* multiple times in *Pakistan*. He has also given *Tafsir Ul Quran* in *Urdu, Pashto,* and English in the United States. It includes *Usul Ul Fiqh, Usul Ul Mirath, Hadith al Qudsi, Hadith an Nabawi* in English on multiple occasions. He considers himself a student to continue acquisitions of knowledge. He is currently leading *Tafsir Ul Quran, Usual Al Fiqh, Seerat Un Nabi,* Science of Inheritance (*Mirath*) in English and *Al Mukhtar Lil Fatawa, Dirayat Ul Riwaya* in *Arabic* in Los Angeles, California.

www.ingramcontent.com/pod-product-compliance
Lightning Source LLC
Chambersburg PA
CBHW020931180426
43192CB00035B/348